Hits and Misses

were songs and recordings, and in this book, I examine these artistic endeavors through the lens of textual criticism, a form of criticism that analyzes and evaluates texts in a detailed way. The study takes as its subject Top 40 singles released between 1963 and 1971 in the USA, Britain, and Canada and considers both the songs themselves and the transformation of those songs in the studio. Thus the book discusses texts and performances and contemplates the relationships between author, text, performance, and audience in order to delineate the creative process as it unfolds from the initial conception of a song to the final mix presented on disc. In other words, *Hits and Misses* investigates the methods by which recordists (songwriters, arrangers, band members, producers, and engineers) impart their ideas to audiences.

As a writer on music, I have always contextualized my work within the culture that produced the texts chosen for study, and in my research on popular music, I prefer to place the musical activities of pop/rock artists in a framework that resonates with popular musicians.[1] Consequently, the methodologies employed in the book are rooted not in cultural studies, semiotics, poststructuralism, Schenkerian techniques, psychology, or sociology but in close readings of texts that, to paraphrase Theodore Gracyk (1996: xiv), square with the views of the musicians themselves. In fact, writers such as Albin Zak (2001: xiii) and Stephen Blum (1992: 213) regard musicians as the best guides to the study of musical practices, and Adam Krims (2000: 29) further argues that musical organization must be taken seriously, precisely because artists, the music industry, and listeners take it seriously.

Hence, my treatment of lyrics draws its methodology and vocabulary from the writings of professional lyricists and focuses on the technical devices songwriters use to enhance the appeal of their narrative structures. Both Sheila Davis (1985) and Jimmy Webb (1998) borrow terms and concepts from classical rhetoric to teach their craft to students, and other songwriters, such as Randy Bachman (Einarson and Bachman

Introduction

In the Top 40 world of the 1960s, the lure of commercial success enticed many musicians into recording studios, where they focused their creative energies on transforming raw songs into musical discourse suitable for phonographic reproduction. The performances these artists committed to tape enhanced the stories they told in their lyrics through a web of interpretive gestures designed to engender, sustain, increase, or resolve emotional and musical tension, the ebb and flow of which established the sonic surfaces of the recordings they released. But once their musical creations had been stamped in vinyl, the expressive elements embedded in the grooves of those discs had to appeal to large numbers of listeners if the records were to score hits instead of misses. Indeed, the sounds emanating from the loudspeakers in record players had become not only the main form of communication between artists and listeners but also the central factor in determining the success or failure of a single.

For musicians in the 1960s, then, the primary texts of popular music

Contents

2011

The Continuum International Publishing Group
80 Maiden Lane, New York, NY 10038
The Tower Building, 11 York Road, London SE1 7NX

www.continuumbooks.com

Library of Congress Cataloging in Publication Data
Toft, Robert.
Hits and misses: crafting top 40 singles, 1963–1971 / by Robert Toft.
    p. cm.
  Includes bibliographical references and index.
  ISBN-13: 978–0–8264–2321–4 (hbk.: alk. paper)
  ISBN-10: 0–8264–2321–3 (hbk.: alk. paper)
  ISBN-13: 978–0–8264–3216–2 (pbk.: alk. paper)
  ISBN-10: 0–8264–3216–6 (pbk.: alk. paper) 1. Popular music—
1961–1970—History and criticism. I. Title.
  ML3470.T64 2010
  781.6409'046—dc22   2010004156

ISBN: 978-0-8264-2321-4 (Hardback)
         978-0-8264-3216-2 (Paperback)

Typeset by Pindar NZ, Auckland, New Zealand
Printed in the United States of America by Thomson-Shore, Inc

Hits and Misses

Crafting Top 40 Singles, 1963–1971

Robert Toft

continuum

2000), speak of an approach to songwriting that directly parallels the art of rhetoric, particularly with regard to invention (*inventio*) and arrangement (*dispositio*). Moreover, I use Bachman's procedure for finding and arranging material as the methodological basis for a discussion of the creative process that leads to the transformation of a song in the recording studio. Similarly, the chapter on harmony places chord progressions in a theoretical framework derived from the modal practices of guitarist-songwriters instead of a system of functional tonality foreign to most popular musicians, and the sections on melodic and vocal style root their discussions in principles extracted directly from recordings. If we strive to work within the musical culture that produced the texts we study, perhaps our scholarly work will become relevant to popular musicians. Otherwise, we might continue to receive the sorts of comments that Tom Constanten of the Grateful Dead directed at Graeme Boone's analytical essay on "Dark Star": "the paper sounds like a weather report in French, delivered perfectly by someone who doesn't speak a word of the language" (Boone 1997: 205).

Part I of the book concentrates on the songs themselves and examines both lyrics and music. "Telling a Story" explores the strategies songwriters employ in developing narratives and the technical devices (especially, figurative language) they use to enrich the telling of those stories. Particular attention is paid to the linear progression of emotional events across the standard "spans of meaning" (verse, chorus, and bridge) that comprise the common song forms of the 1960s. The second chapter, "Prosodic Tunes," considers melodic line from the perspective of prosody and the natural delivery of words and treats melodic style as a function of vocal delivery. Accentuation within words and the emphasis placed on words in phrases often determines the rhythmic structure of a vocal melody, and by comparing several performances of the same song ("Try a Little Tenderness"), one can observe how singers transform a pre-existing tune. "Guitar-Based Modalities," the final chapter of the section, places the harmonic style of pop/rock in a flexible framework that comprehends both scales and chord progressions from within the idiomatic nature of guitar playing, as well as the processes of songwriting and recording. The harmonic palette of popular music from the mid and late 1960s undoubtedly owes much of its distinctive character to the musical habits of guitarists, for these musicians frequently exploit easily negotiable hand positions to produce riffs and chord progressions that comfortably fit their instrument.

The second part of the book investigates the sonic surface of recordings and considers how recordists fashion musical material into effective musical discourse. The vocal track is probably the most prominent feature of a Top 40 single, and a discussion of the expressive style of singing captured on tape leads to three case studies that contemplate the inter-relationship of performance, timbre, texture, and expressive flow, the latter a term I use to describe the creation and release of emotional and musical tension. The first chapter of Part II, "Bel Canto: The Unbroken Tradition," treats the pop/rock style of singing as a continuation of older *bel canto* customs and places the vocal techniques and interpretive gestures used in the world of pop/rock on a continuum of practices that extends back to the eighteenth century. "Invention and Arrangement," the initial case study, focuses on The Guess Who's song "Laughing" and delineates the ways recordists discover and then structure musical ideas to create an effective musical discourse. It positions the method of songwriting adopted by Randy Bachman and Burton Cummings within the larger context of rhetorical construction and reveals just how attentive the recordists were to arrangement. The next chapter, "Transforming a Demo," considers the art of turning an unpretentious demo into a powerful musical discourse and concentrates on "Behind Blue Eyes" by The Who, exploring not only the evolution of the track as the recordists work toward the final mix released on *Who's Next* but also the distribution of musical ideas and instruments within the three versions available for scrutiny. The final chapter, "Hit-and-Miss Affair," evaluates three recordings of Burt Bacharach and Hal David's "(They Long to Be) Close to You" and investigates the hit-and-miss nature of crafting singles through an analysis of Bacharach and David's two misses (one with Richard Chamberlain and the other with Dionne Warwick) and an assessment of the Carpenters' hit. Specifically, it considers how groove, instrumentation, melodic style, tempo, manner of performance (both vocal and instrumental), and the disposition of the song's sections (verses and bridge) generate an expressive flow that either enhances or diminishes the emotional impact of the story told in the lyrics.

All these discussions assume a modest technical background in music, and if readers are to benefit fully from the book, they may wish to listen to the recordings listed in the discography at the appropriate time. The fifth chapter of the book first appeared in "Rhetorical Criticism and the Creative Process: Invention and Arrangement in The Guess Who's 'Laughing'," *Proceedings of The Art of Record Production Conference 2005* (http://www.artofrecordproduction.com) and the seventh chapter in "Hits and Misses: Crafting a Pop Single for the Top-40 Market in the 1960s," *Popular Music* 29 (2010): 267–81.

Acknowledgements

I wish to thank The University of Western Ontario, especially Ted Hewitt (Vice-President, Research and International Relations), for a grant that covered the cost of obtaining permission from the companies listed below to reprint lyrics and/or music from the following songs:

Lyric by Hal David

Music by Burt Bacharach

Copyright © 1968 (Renewed) Casa David and New Hidden Valley
Music

International Copyright Secured   All Rights Reserved

Reprinted by permission of Hal Leonard Corporation

Laughing

Words and Music by Randy Bachman and Burton Cummings

© 1969 (Renewed 1997) SHILLELAGH MUSIC (SOCAN/BMI)/
Administered by BUG MUSIC

This arrangement © 2010 SHILLELAGH MUSIC (SOCAN/BMI)/
Administered by BUG MUSIC

All Rights Reserved   Used by Permission

Reprinted by permission of Hal Leonard Corporation

The Look Of Love

From CASINO ROYALE

Words by Hal David

Music by Burt Bacharach

© 1967 (Renewed 1995) COLGEMS-EMI MUSIC INC.

All Rights Reserved   International Copyright Secured   Used by
Permission

Reprinted by permission of Hal Leonard Corporation

Ode To Billie Joe

Words and Music by BOBBIE GENTRY

© 1967 (Renewed) NORTHRIDGE MUSIC COMPANY

All Rights Administered by UNIVERSAL MUSIC CORPORATION
(Publishing) and ALFRED MUSIC PUBLISHING CO., INC.
(Print)

(Sittin' On) The Dock Of The Bay
Words and Music by Steve Cropper and Otis Redding

(There's) Always Something There To Remind Me
Lyric by Hal David
Music by Burt Bacharach

(They Long To Be) Close To You [acknowledgement for reprinting
    music]
Words and Music by Burt Bacharach and Hal David

(They Long To Be) Close To You [acknowledgement for reprinting
    lyrics]
Lyric by Hal David
Music by Burt Bacharach

Part I

THE SONG

Chapter 1

Telling a Story

Words have an enormous capacity to move people deeply, and when words, in the form of lyrics, are combined with music, songwriters have the perfect vehicle for penetrating the minds and emotions of listeners not only through the stories they tell but also through the music they compose to enhance the impact of those stories. Finely crafted lyrics often transform personal experiences or observations on the human condition into narratives that are designed to appeal to large numbers of listeners, and because the scope for dramatic development in pop singles of the 1960s was limited to three or four minutes, story lines had to progress quickly and efficiently to satisfy listeners. Professional songwriters from the era were certainly well aware of the restrictions placed on them, for Jimmy Webb, in his book *Tunesmith: Inside the Art of Songwriting*, advises lyricists to confine their "little radio plays" to "one or two characters . . . and perhaps fifty seconds for each act. We have to get while the getting's good" (1998: 38). Thus songwriters active in the 1960s worked in miniature, and their lyrics frequently center on the development of a single thought, idea, or emotion.

Listeners assimilate the narrative through a structure in which words are organized into dramatic "spans of meaning" (Webb 1998: 80),[1] and each one of these spans engenders, sustains, increases, or resolves tension (Davis 1985: 23). In other words, the various sections of a song (verse, chorus, and bridge) contribute to the emotional ebb and flow of the drama as it unfolds. Songwriters usually adopt a conversational tone in these little radio plays, and they often construct their lyrics to give the impression that the listener is overhearing a private conversation.[2] The details of this conversation, as well as the emotions central to the drama, are revealed in a linear fashion across several spans of meaning that lead the listener to the emotional climax of the song.

Standard arrangements of these spans of meaning became the norm in the 1960s, and most songs from the decade follow (or are based on) one of four patterns: a series of verses, verses with a chorus, verses with a bridge, or verses with both a chorus and a bridge. A verse is a lyrical and musical unit comprised of several phrases or lines organized into a paragraph of thought, and in strophic songs or ballads, as they are also known, the musical elements remain the same from verse to verse while the lyric content changes. Songwriters frequently embellished this basic structure by adding a refrain, a textual/musical phrase that punctuates the story line at the end of each verse as an integral part of the unit. A chorus, on the other hand, functions differently from a refrain, because a chorus is a separate entity of contrasting text and music that is repeated (usually in unaltered form) at regular intervals during a song. It often contains musical and/or textual hooks and may be preceded by a short section, normally two to four lines of text, which sets the stage for it. This preparatory section, known as the lead-in or pre-chorus, is usually embedded in the verse as its final lines, and if a lead-in is present in the first verse, it is typically found in subsequent verses. A bridge, however, provides a unique lyrical and musical departure within a song, and songwriters frequently place it between two statements of the chorus. Many recordings of the 1960s frame these standard spans of meaning with opening and closing instrumental sections (intro and outro), but the closing section of a recording may also be based on the last textual unit of the song (commonly the chorus) and may include a repeated idea that is faded out to end the recording.

A multitude of songs exemplify the principles songwriters employ in crafting lyrics, and I have chosen a small number of representative works to illustrate various strategies of story development. These songs range from conventional ballads and verse/chorus/bridge structures to those that vary customary procedures somewhat:

Ballad: "By the Time I Get to Phoenix," Jimmy Webb
Ballad with refrain: "Ode to Billie Joe," Bobbie Gentry
Verses with chorus: "Both Sides, Now," Joni Mitchell
Verses with bridge: "Here, There and Everywhere," John Lennon and
    Paul McCartney
Verses with lead-in, chorus, bridge: "You've Lost That Lovin' Feelin',"
    Barry Mann, Phil Spector, Cynthia Weil.

Jimmy Webb's "By the Time I Get to Phoenix," a Top 40 hit for Glen Campbell in 1967, employs simple ballad form to tell a poignant story across three verses (see Example 1). The commonplace subject of the song, the jilted lover, centers on a single emotional event presented in an innovative way. In Webb's own words, the song opens with a teaser ("by the time I get to Phoenix, she'll be risin'"), an ambiguous situation meant to pique the curiosity of the listener: "we don't know who is speaking and we don't know about whom he's speaking, but we do know that he's on his way to Phoenix, presumably in the early hours of the morning since by the time he arrives there another person — a woman — will have awakened and will be leaving her bed" (1998: 40). The subsequent lines begin to build the story through specific details that establish the characters and dramatic situation of this little radio play. The story, we learn, focuses on the breakup of a relationship told from the male protagonist's perspective as he leaves town. Each span of meaning is complete in itself, and Webb amplifies the emotional line through an incremental progression of ideas and events (the rhetorical figure *incrementum*) that follows the journeys of the protagonists both geographically and chronologically.

Example 1.   "By the Time I Get to Phoenix," Jimmy Webb (words and timings from the 1967 recording by Glen Campbell)

0:00	*Intro*	[instrumental]
0:11	*Verse 1*	By the time I get to Phoenix, she'll be risin'
		She'll find the note I left hangin' on her door
		She'll laugh when she reads the part that says I'm leavin'
		'Cause I've left that girl so many times before
0:54	*Verse 2*	By the time I make Albuquerque, she'll be workin'
		She'll prob'ly stop at lunch and give me a call
		But she'll just hear that phone keep on ringin'
		Off the wall, that's all
1:38	*Verse 3*	By the time I make Oklahoma, she'll be sleepin'
		She'll turn softly and call my name out low
		And she'll cry just to think I'd really leave her
		Though time and time I've tried to tell her so
2:20	*Extension*	She just didn't know I would really go
2:32	*Outro*	[repeated instrumental figure with fade]
2:39	*track ends*	

Incrementum involves the amplification of a subject through a continuous and unbroken series of steps in which each new idea or word is stronger than the last, or as Henry Peacham defined the device centuries ago, *incrementum* is a "scaling ladder, by which [orators] climb to the top of high comparison" (1593: 169).[3] On each step of this ladder, Webb places a verse, and as Sheila Davis points out (1985: 36–37), the first lines of the verses not only trace the male protagonist's journey from Phoenix to Albuquerque to Oklahoma but also chronicle the female protagonist's day from rising to working to sleeping. This arrangement of the material heightens the emotional intensity of the drama from one verse to the next in a logical series of events. In the first verse, the woman rises, finds the note, and laughs, and in the second verse, she works, stops and calls, and hears the phone continue ringing. In the third verse, the emotional peak of the song, she sleeps, turns and calls, and then cries because she suddenly realizes that the man she (presumably) loves has actually left her. The one-line extension to this verse reinforces the stark reality of the situation from the perspective of the male protagonist — "she just didn't know I would really go."

Several other technical devices help Webb tell his story eloquently. He places the rhetorical figure *anaphora*, that is, the repetition of the same word or group of words at the beginning of successive clauses,[4] in each verse to propel both the story and emotional lines forward:

I She'll be risin'
She'll find the note
She'll laugh
II She'll be workin'
She'll prob'ly stop
But she'll just hear
III She'll be sleepin'

> She'll turn softly
>
> And she'll cry

This figure unifies the lyrical thought while simultaneously introducing new details of the story in a series of steps that generates a ladder within each verse (in addition to the ladder between the verses). *Polyptoton*, the repetition of a stem word with a variation in case,[5] adorns the third and fourth lines of the first verse, and the graceful interplay of cases in close proximity (leavin'/left) creates a sound effect that artfully varies the conversational tone of the lyric. But beyond the use of figurative language to heighten the effect of the story, Webb's deployment of rhyme allows the climax to land with greater force. In the first two verses, he establishes the pattern *a b a b*, but in the third verse, he changes the rhyme scheme to *a b c b*. This subtly draws attention to the climactic peak of the song, the third line of the stanza ("and she'll cry just to think I'd really leave her"):

I	risin'	*a*		II	workin'	*a*		III	sleepin'	*a*
	door	*b*			call	*b*			low	*b*
	leavin'	*a*			ringin'	*a*			her	*c*
	before	*b*			all	*b*			so	*b*

Webb's finely crafted lyric tells a simple story derived from a single emotion that has been illustrated through a set of circumstances arranged, as Webb says himself, in "a fully realized scenario that reveals in careful, logical stages the true goal or intent of the writer" (1998: 40). Other ballads from the 1960s follow a similar plan, but in many of them, songwriters incorporate a refrain to reinforce an idea central to their narrative.

"Ode to Billie Joe," an explosive hit for Bobbie Gentry in the summer of 1967, employs ballad/refrain form to tell an enigmatic story of suicide in the Mississippi Delta. In the opening lines, Gentry works efficiently to set the scene in which her drama will unfold. She first establishes the time and place of the story and then introduces the narrator, who is at work with her brother on the family farm (see Example 2). They stop at dinnertime and walk back to the house to eat, where their mother tells them, quite casually, that Billie Joe McAllister has jumped off the Tallahatchie Bridge. Gentry turns the line bearing this news, the last line of the verse, into a refrain, and as the story develops, she uses the refrain as a vehicle to heighten the mystery surrounding Billie Joe's death.

Example 2.   "Ode To Billie Joe," Bobbie Gentry (words and timings from her 1967 recording)

0:00	*Intro*	[instrumental]
0:08	*Verse 1*	It was the third of June, another sleepy, dusty Delta day
		I was out choppin' cotton and my brother was balin' hay
		And at dinner time we stopped and walked back to the house to eat
		And Mama hollered out the back door, "Y'all remember to wipe your feet"
		And then she said, "I got some news this mornin' from Choctaw Ridge
		Today Billie Joe McAllister jumped off the Tallahatchie Bridge"
0:57	*Verse 2*	n' Papa said to Mama as he passed around the black-eyed peas
		"Well Billie Joe never had a lick of sense, pass the biscuits, please
		There's five more acres in the lower forty I got to plow"
		And Mama said it was shame about Billie Joe, anyhow

Seems like nothin' ever comes to no good up on
Choctaw Ridge
And now Billie Joe McAllister's jumped off the
Tallahatchie Bridge

1:44 *Verse 3*   n' Brother said he recollected when he and Tom
and Billie Joe
Put a frog down my back at the Carroll County
picture show
"And wasn't I talkin' to him after church last
Sunday night?
I'll have another piece of apple pie, you know it
don't seem right
I saw him at the sawmill yesterday on Choctaw
Ridge
And now you tell me Billie Joe's jumped off the
Tallahatchie Bridge"

2:31 *Verse 4*   n' Mama said to me, "Child, what's happened to
your appetite?
I've been cookin' all mornin' and you haven't
touched a single bite
That nice young preacher, Brother Taylor, dropped
by today
Said he'd be pleased to have dinner on Sunday, oh,
by the way
He said he saw a girl that looked a lot like you up
on Choctaw Ridge
And she and Billie Joe was throwin' somethin' off
the Tallahatchie Bridge"

3:19 *Verse 5*   A year has come n' gone since we heard the news
'bout Billie Joe
n' Brother married Becky Thompson, they bought
a store in Tupelo

There was a virus goin' 'round, Papa caught it and
        he died last spring
And now Mama doesn't seem to wanna do much
        of anything
And me, I spend a lot of time pickin' flowers up on
        Choctaw Ridge
And drop them into the muddy water off the
        Tallahatchie Bridge

4:03   *Outro*   [instrumental]
4:12   *track ends*

Over lunch, the narrator is curiously silent while the rest of the family discusses, almost indifferently, the suicide and their recent interactions with Billie Joe. The reason for the narrator's silence gradually becomes apparent in the next verse, the emotional climax of the song, when the mother, noticing that her daughter (the narrator) hasn't touched her food, mentions that Brother Taylor had visited and had seen Billie Joe and a girl who looked like her daughter throwing something off the Tallahatchie Bridge. Clearly, the narrator was more than casually involved with Billie Joe, for she is upset enough by the news of his death to have lost her appetite, and the revelation that she and Billie Joe were on the Tallahatchie Bridge shortly before the suicide introduced a mystery that helped keep the song in the number one position on the *Billboard* charts for four weeks: what did Billie Joe and the narrator throw off the bridge and why did Billie Joe then kill himself? The fifth and final verse does not answer these questions but transports the listener to the vantage point from where the story is told. A year has passed and not only has the narrator's brother married but also her father has died of a virus. Both of the women in the story are left to mourn their losses, the mother not wanting to do "much of anything" and the narrator spending a great deal of time picking flowers and dropping them into the water off the Tallahatchie Bridge.

Gentry's haunting tale of suicide and a family's reaction to it suits the expansive nature of ballad form well (the song clocks in at 4 minutes and 12 seconds), and the transformation of the refrain from a static line contrived to reinforce the central theme of the narrative in the first three verses to a dynamic force that contributes to the enigmatic appeal of the lyrics in verses four and five strengthens the emotional impact of the song. A similar procedure occurs in certain verse/chorus structures, and in "Both Sides, Now," Joni Mitchell adapts the words of the chorus to parallel the argument as it unfolds.

"Both Sides, Now" tells its story not through the type of direct development common in ballads but through three inter-related vignettes arranged to lead the listener in stepwise fashion from a reflection on clouds, to a contemplation of love, to a consideration of life (see Example 3). This method of amplification, similar to the *incrementum* employed by Jimmy Webb in "By the Time I Get to Phoenix," allows ideas to progress in logical stages so that subsequent sections further the dramatic situation of the previous segments. Each vignette (two verses and a chorus) presents a self-contained span of meaning, and the first two use metaphoric descriptions of clouds and love as rungs on an emotional ladder. In the third section, the climax of the song, Mitchell draws together sentiments from the previous two vignettes to intensify the drama ("dreams and schemes" from the first and "tears and fears" from the second). Here, the metaphoric imagery gives way to a climactic emotional event, "to say 'I love you' right out loud," a personal act well within the direct experience of every listener.

Mitchell unifies this long, compartmentalized structure with the parallel application of *antithesis* (the comparison of contrary persons or things). In all three sections, a pair of contrasting verses prepares the listener for the conclusion drawn in the chorus, the first verse considering the positive attributes of the subject and the second dwelling on the negative. The chorus then brings together the contrary notions outlined in the verses ("I've looked at [clouds, love, life] from both sides now") and comments on the illusory nature of the subject at hand ("it's [cloud, love's, life's] illusions I recall"), before concluding that one really can't know clouds, love, or life at all. In addition to this form of symmetrical construction, Mitchell furthers the parallelism of her verses in three other ways. She incorporates internal rhyme in the first line of each vignette ("*rows* and *floes* of angel hair," "*moons* and *Junes* and Ferris wheels," and "*tears* and *fears* and feeling proud"), ushers in the antithetical nature of the second verses with the words "but now," and ends every verse with either an identical or a closely matched word (way, away, day).

Example 3. "Both Sides, Now," Joni Mitchell (words and timings from her 1969 recording)

0:00	*Intro*	[instrumental]
0:11	*Verse 1*	Rows and floes of angel hair
		And ice cream castles in the air
		And feather canyons ev'rywhere
		I've looked at clouds that way
0:30	*Verse 2*	But now they only block the sun
		They rain and snow on ev'ryone
		So many things I would have done
		But clouds got in my way
0:50	*Chorus 1*	I've looked at clouds from both sides now
		From up and down, and still somehow
		It's cloud illusions I recall
		I really don't know clouds at all
1:22	*Verse 3*	Moons and Junes and Ferris wheels
		The dizzy dancing way you feel
		As ev'ry fairy tale comes real
		I've looked at love that way
1:42	*Verse 4*	But now it's just another show
		You leave 'em laughing when you go

		And if you care, don't let them know
		Don't give yourself away
2:01	*Chorus 2*	I've looked at love from both sides now
		From give and take, and still somehow
		It's love's illusions I recall
		I really don't know love at all
2:33	*Verse 5*	Tears and fears and feeling proud
		To say "I love you" right out loud
		Dreams and schemes and circus crowds
		I've looked at life that way
2:53	*Verse 6*	But now old friends are acting strange
		They shake their heads, they say I've changed
		Well something's lost, but something's gained
		In living ev'ry day
3:13	*Chorus 3*	I've looked at life from both sides now
		From win and lose and still somehow
		It's life's illusions I recall
		I really don't know life at all
3:44	*Chorus 4*	I've looked at life from both sides now
		From up and down, and still somehow
		It's life's illusions I recall
		I really don't know life at all
4:16	*Outro*	[instrumental]
4:31	*track ends*	

But beyond these structural devices, Mitchell adorns her text with figurative language that helps elevate it from the commonplace. The subtle variation of a stem word to form the figure *polyptoton* (living/life in lines 32 and 33) adds harmonious grace to the lyric's climactic moment, and in the first two vignettes, Mitchell draws her positive imagery from uniformly metaphoric word palettes. Clouds are described as angel hair, ice cream castles, and feather canyons, whereas love is likened to Ferris wheels, dizzy dancing, and fairy tales (Davis 1985: 93). The choruses, on the other hand, employ localized *antithesis* to summarize the opposing sentiments expressed in the verses ("up and down," "give and take," "win and lose"), and in the final vignette, *antithesis* permeates not only the chorus but also the verses themselves. At first, Mitchell contrasts "tears and fears" with "dreams and schemes," and in the next verse, the antithetical nature of "something's lost, but something's gained" foreshadows the contrariety of the chorus's "win and lose."

Mitchell's meticulously crafted lyric, replete with figures intended to structure the argument as well as delight the ear, utilizes verse/chorus form to tell a story of love and life through a series of meditations. The metaphoric teaser that opens the first vignette sets the stage for the contrasting second verse, and the chorus, in addition to reinforcing the antithetical treatment of the subject, encapsulates the central theme of the song with the phrase "both sides now." But as the lyric progresses, Mitchell adjusts the chorus to suit each vignette and in the process creates the connective tissue that binds the various strands of the story together. In essence, her choruses are both a direct consequence of the verses immediately preceding them and a summation of the entire song, for they regularly focus the listener's attention on the imponderability of life in all its complexity (Davis 1985: 54). In other types of narratives, however, the inclusion of a bridge, a single span of meaning designed to expand the emotional dimension of the lyric, may be more appropriate for the development of a story than the regular affirmation of the predominant message.

Lennon and McCartney certainly use verse/bridge form effectively in "Here, There and Everywhere," for the bridge they fashion, in addition to providing contrasting lyrical and musical content, represents the emotional climax of the story (see Example 4). The lyric begins with a teaser that functions as a prologue and ends with an epilogue that brings together in one place salient points dispersed throughout the song. The teaser, "to lead a better life, I need my love to be here," takes the form of a *propositio* (a general statement that sets forth in a few words the sum of the matter being presented), and the following three spans of meaning deal with aspects of the proposition in a logical progression from "here" (verse 1) to "there" (verse 2) to "everywhere" (bridge). This arrangement allows Lennon and McCartney to detail the various ways one person can enrich the life of another in a structure that ascends by degrees to the top of the matter. In other words, they amplify the statement under consideration ("to lead a better life") through a series of continuous and unbroken steps in which each new unit is stronger than the last.

Example 4.   "Here, There and Everywhere," John Lennon and Paul McCartney (words and timings from the 1966 recording by The Beatles)

0:00	*Prologue*	To lead a better life, I need my love to be here
0:10	*Verse 1*	Here, making each day of the year
		Changing my life with a wave of her hand
		Nobody can deny that there's something there
0:33	*Verse 2*	There, running my hands through her hair
		Both of us thinking how good it can be
		Someone is speaking but she doesn't know he's there
0:55	*Bridge*	I want her everywhere and if she's beside me
		I know I need never care
		But to love her is to need her
1:08	*Verse 3*	Everywhere, knowing that love is to share
		Each one believing that love never dies
		Watching her eyes and hoping I'm always there
1:29	*Bridge*	I want her everywhere and if she's beside me
		I know I need never care
		But to love her is to need her
1:42	*Verse 3*	Everywhere, knowing that love is to share
		Each one believing that love never dies
		Watching her eyes and hoping I'm always there

2:05   *Epilogue*   I will be there and everywhere

                 Here, there and everywhere

2:21   *track ends*

Localized figurative language reinforces this superstructure, for Lennon and McCartney connect the opening units of the story by means of *anadiplosis*, a figure in which the last word of one phrase becomes the first word of the next, and this device, like all figures of repetition, furthers the argument as much through pleasantness of sound as through a stepwise increase in the emotional line of the story:

> To lead a better life, I need my love to be *here*
>
> *Here*, making each day of the year
> Changing my life with a wave of her hand
> Nobody can deny that there's something *there*
>
> *There*, running my hands through her hair
> Both of us thinking how good it can be
> Someone is speaking but she doesn't know he's *there*.

But the songwriters do more than propel their lyric forward with *anadiplosis*, for they frame the second verse with *epanalepsis*, a unit that begins and ends with the same word or words. This figure places a word of importance at the beginning of a section to be considered and in the end to be remembered, and the use of it in the second verse not only signals the close of this portion of the argument but also leads listeners to expect some sort of new event.[6] This expectation is fulfilled in the musical and lyrical excursion that follows. In the bridge, the graduated climb from "here" to "there" reaches a climax when the speaker realizes that he needs his companion not just "here" and "there" but "everywhere."

The last verse of the song functions in a way similar to a dénouement, and it is joined to the bridge through a device in which a single word ("everywhere") serves more than one clause. The pleasing effect produced by this technique not only helps release the tension created in the climax but also provides a seamless transition to the dénouement, and in this final span of meaning, Lennon and McCartney particularize the notion of "everywhere" with references to the immortality of a shared love. The reprise of the interlocked bridge and dénouement which follows re-emphasizes the climax and leads to an epilogue that employs the figure *frequentatio* (when points dispersed throughout a passage are brought together in one place) to draw together in encapsulated form the ideas associated with "here," "there," and "everywhere."

Paul McCartney is far too modest when he comments to his biographer Barry Miles that the song has "a couple of interesting structural points about it: lyrically the way it combines the whole title: each verse takes a word. 'Here' discusses here. Next verse, 'there' discusses there, then it pulls it all together in the last verse, with 'everywhere'" (Miles 1997: 286). This carefully constructed lyric combines a traditional verse/bridge structure with novel figurative devices to tell a compelling story of the love an individual can find with another person. The opening teaser speaks of leading a better life through love, but the converse of this, the dissolution of love already found, has also been a subject of enduring interest to songwriters, and in The Righteous Brothers' hit from 1965, "You've Lost That Lovin' Feelin'," both a bridge and chorus were necessary for the composers, Barry Mann, Phil Spector, and Cynthia Weil, to turn an intensely personal experience into an appealing narrative.

"You've Lost That Lovin' Feelin'" presents an intimate story of a disintegrating love affair in a manner reminiscent of a soliloquy. Listeners overhear a private, one-sided conversation during which the singer, as protagonist, comes to realize that the subtle changes he has noticed in his lover's behavior are clear signs of her reduced feelings for him. Right at the outset, a simple observation by the protagonist ("you never close your eyes anymore when I kiss your lips") not only establishes the emotional situation of this little radio play but also puts listeners, as Jimmy Webb has noted, on an extremely intimate footing with both the singer and the object of his desire (1998: 42). The protagonist's second observation, which focuses on his lover's lack of tenderness, amplifies the circumstances surrounding the interaction of the two characters and prepares the ground for the lead-in embedded at the end of the verse. Here, the singer momentarily reflects on his situation ("you're trying hard not to show it, but baby I know it"), before drawing the inescapable conclusion that his lover has indeed lost her feelings for him. This chain of reasoning, personal observations followed by reflection on them, builds directly to the main expository statement of the song, "you've lost that lovin' feelin'," and the chorus is the natural place for this type of linear development to reach an emotional peak. The songwriters further intensify the impact of the singer's conclusion by repeating the title line and emphasizing the word "gone" through *epizeuxis* (the immediate repetition of a word to draw attention to the state of mind associated with that word).

Example 5.   "You've Lost That Lovin' Feelin'," Barry Mann, Phil Spector, and Cynthia Weil (words and timings from the 1965 recording by The Righteous Brothers)

0:00	*Verse 1*	You never close your eyes
		Anymore when I kiss your lips
		And there's no tenderness
		Like before in your fingertips
0:21	*Lead-in*	You're trying hard not to show it (baby)
		But baby, baby I know it
0:32	*Chorus 1*	You've lost that lovin' feelin'
		Wooo, that lovin' feelin'
		You've lost that lovin' feelin'

		Now it's gone, gone, gone, wooo
0:57	*Verse 2*	Now there's no welcome look
		In your eyes when I reach for you
		And now you're starting to
		Criticize little things I do
1:17	*Lead-in*	It makes me just feel like crying (baby)
		Cause baby, something beautiful's dyin'
1:29	*Chorus 2*	You've lost that lovin' feelin'
		Wooo, that lovin' feelin'
		You've lost that lovin' feelin'
		Now it's gone, gone, gone, wooo
1:55	*Bridge*	Baby, baby, I'd get down on my knees for you
		If you would only love me like you used to do, yeah
		We had a love, a love, a love you don't find everyday
		So don't, don't, don't, don't let it slip away
2:35		Baby (baby), baby (baby), I beg of you please (please), please (please)
		I need your love (I need your love), I need your love (I need your love)
		So bring it on back (so bring it on back)
		Bring it on back (so bring it on back)
2:55	*Chorus 3*	Bring back that lovin' feelin'
		Wooo, that lovin' feelin'
		Bring back that lovin' feelin'
		Cause it's gone, gone, gone
		And I can't go on, wooo
3:25	*Fade*	Bring back that lovin' feelin'
		Wooo, that lovin' feelin'
		Bring back that lovin' feelin'
		Cause it's gone, gone, gone
3:45	*track ends*	

In the second verse, two additional observations deepen the singer's understanding of his deteriorating situation and evoke a heart-felt response from him: "It makes me just feel like cryin', cause baby something beautiful's dyin'." These lines return listeners to the emotional intensity of the first chorus, but the song has not yet reached its most climactic point, for in the latter part of the bridge which follows, the main expository statement is broadened into a desperate plea. An initial brief respite from the emotional turmoil of the verse/chorus structure ("I'd get down on my knees for you, if you would only love me like you used to do"), the proverbial lull before the storm, prepares listeners for the protagonist's agitated plea uttered from bended knee ("I beg you please, I need your love, so bring it on back"). The final chorus subsides slightly from this heightened emotional state and functions as a resolution to the protagonist's predicament — all he can do is hope that her feelings for him will return. The songwriters link these important dramatic moments through *anadiplosis*, the last words of the climactic peak ("bring it on back") becoming the first words of the dénouement ("bring back that lovin' feelin'").

"You've Lost That Lovin' Feelin'" skillfully tells a story of disintegrating love across several spans of meaning which either engender, sustain, increase, or resolve tension. The arrangement of these spans in an order that deftly combines an exposition of details with rising action creates a satisfying emotional ebb and flow in which each span is a natural consequence of the preceding section. The first four lines of the verses illustrate and amplify the emotional viewpoint of the protagonist, while the two lead-ins extend and increase tension by reaching up to a higher emotional level. The choruses then present the main expository statement of the song and sustain the energy achieved in the lead-ins. The bridge, positioned about three-quarters of the way through the song, provides new insight into the protagonist's emotions, and because it portrays the singer at his most intense and yet most vulnerable moment, represents the climax of this little radio play. A graphic reduction of the emotional line of the story clearly reveals the care with which the songwriters constructed the architecture of their drama, and in the following graph, the story is represented as a series of emotional events that unfold across the song (see Example 6).

Example 6.   Emotional stages of "You've Lost That Lovin' Feelin'"[7]

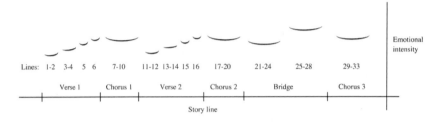

Linear progressions of emotional events, especially when they are placed within unambiguous structures, allow listeners to assimilate meaning effortlessly, and the songs discussed in this chapter utilize common forms to turn personal experiences and observations on the human condition into fully realized scenarios that have universal appeal. The ideas presented in these songs penetrate the minds and emotions of listeners not only through the stories songwriters tell but also through the music they compose, and since melodic style frequently enhances the natural delivery of words, the next chapter explores the prosodic relationship between tunes and words.

Chapter 2

Prosodic Tunes

The final shaping of melodic lines has always been the prerogative of performers, and in the Top 40 world of the 1960s, singers tended to deliver words in a natural manner that molded melodies to the patterns of speech. In fact, the old *bel canto* axiom from the nineteenth century, "sing every word with the same accent and emphasis as you would speak it" (Kitchiner 1821: 70), seems to have been such an important guiding principle for many pop/rock singers that the melodic style of the 1960s may be viewed as much as a function of vocal delivery as of compositional intent. Historically, that is, in the *bel canto* era of the late eighteenth and early nineteenth centuries, vocalists aligned singing with speaking by attending to the "laws of prosody," and this approach required the accents, emphases, pauses, and syllabic quantities of normal speech to be keenly observed in singing (Hamilton 1853: 20).[1] Accent referred to the stress laid on syllables and emphasis to the force placed on important words so they were distinguished above the rest, accent dignifying the syllable and emphasis ennobling the word. Pauses, the blank spaces speakers and singers inserted in the sentences they uttered, organized and paced the delivery of ideas and emotions, and a judicious combination of accent, emphasis, pausing, and syllable length enabled vocalists to create a feeling of spontaneity while personalizing songs to make the sentiments of the words their own.

These four aspects of delivery remain foundational to many styles of singing, and in the twentieth century, just as in earlier times, these techniques helped singers individualize vocal lines. Indeed, pop/rock artists routinely made use of the principles of prosody when personalizing melodies, and a comparison of several performances of a single song demonstrates how singers from divergent vocal traditions transformed a pre-existing tune. The recordings of "Try a Little Tenderness" (Harry Wood, Jimmy Campbell, and Reg Connelly) by Ruth Etting (1933), Bing Crosby (1933 and 1955), Mel Tormé (1946 and 1957), Frank Sinatra (1946 and 1960), Aretha Franklin (1962), Sam Cooke (1964), and Otis Redding (1966) clearly show the differences between the less-prosodic approach associated with both torch singers from the 1930s (Etting) and crooners active in the 1940s and 1950s (Crosby, Sinatra, and Tormé) and the speech-oriented style of performers who first gained popularity in the 1950s or 1960s (Cooke, Franklin, and Redding).

When the Robbins Music Corporation of New York published the slow and torchy "Try a Little Tenderness" in 1933, no one could have predicted that the song would have an enduring appeal to successive generations of listeners. From the first recordings by Ted Lewis, Bing Crosby, and Ruth Etting in 1933 to the versions released by Aretha Franklin in 1962 and Otis Redding in 1966, the song never went out of fashion, for singers continually adapted it to their performance styles. The original American sheet music consisted of an 8-bar instrumental prelude, marked "slowly with expression," followed by a 16-bar vocal introduction coupled to a verse/verse/bridge/verse structure of 32-bars that carried the rubric "very slow, tenderly" (see Example 1),[2] and right from the beginning of the song's recorded history, performers found ways of altering its shape and tempo. Ted Lewis, for example, not only omitted the opening words to focus on a spoken rendition of the verse/bridge structure but also rendered the song at a quick tempo, as did Bing Crosby. Ruth Etting, on the other hand, adhered closely to the text Robbins had printed. She retained the initial words, delivering them somewhat freely, before she settled on a slow regular pulse for the rest of the song. Later performers, such as Frank Sinatra (1946) and Mel Tormé (1957), also maintained the tempo and shape of the original publication, while Aretha Franklin (1962) and Otis Redding (1966) performed the song slowly but without the opening words. Interestingly, Crosby, Sinatra, and Tormé recorded the song twice, Crosby consistently including the vocal introduction in his recordings (1933 and 1955) and Sinatra and Tormé leaving it out on one of their discs, Sinatra in 1960 and Tormé in 1946. But beyond these two main performance traditions, that is, in addition to readings which either included or excluded the introductory words, a severely truncated version of the song — just the first and last verses — appeared as part of a medley with "For Sentimental Reasons" and "You Send Me" on Sam Cooke's "live" recording made at New York's Copacabana club in 1964.

Example 1.   Lyrics and structure of "Try a Little Tenderness," as published by the Robbins Music Corporation (1933)

Prelude	*Slowly (with expression)*
(8 bars)	[Instrumental]
Vocal Intro	In the hustle of today
(16 bars)	We're all inclined to miss
	Little things that mean so much
	A word, a smile, a kiss
	When a woman loves a man
	He's a hero in her eyes
	And a hero he can always be

	If he'll just realize
Verse 1	*Very slow, tenderly*
(8 bars)	Women do get weary
	Wearing the same shabby dress
	And when she's weary
	Try a little tenderness
Verse 2	You know she's waiting
(8 bars)	Just anticipating
	Things she may never possess
	While she's without them
	Try a little tenderness
Bridge	It's not just sentimental
(8 bars)	She has her grief and care
	And a word that's soft and gentle
	Makes it easier to bear
Verse 3	You won't regret it
(8 bars)	Women don't forget it
	Love is their whole happiness
	It's all so easy
	Try a little tenderness

Within these structural conventions, each singer left an indelible mark on "Try a Little Tenderness," Otis Redding believing that, after listening to the Franklin and Cooke versions prior to recording the song, he had transformed the tune to such an extent that he had invented a "brand new song" (Bowman 2003: 104, 124). Apparently, Redding consciously set out to re-create "Try a Little Tenderness," or as his manager, Phil Walden, told interviewer Rob Bowman, to hear it in such a different way that the song was turned "totally around" (Bowman 2003: 124). The process of individualizing musical material has preoccupied musicians for centuries, and the degree to which performers reshape the music they sing may be placed on a continuum that extends from the minimal alteration of melodies through prosodic interpretation to the wholesale re-creation of the tune's structure. The older generation of singers who recorded "Try a Little Tenderness," particularly Crosby, Etting, Sinatra, and Tormé, lightly personalized, that is, interpreted, the melody by applying the principles of prosody to establish its rhythmic character without redefining the pitch contour in a significant way, whereas the younger generation of singers represented by Franklin and Redding placed prosodic delivery in a tradition which required them to introduce substantial musical modifications so that they could re-create "Try a Little Tenderness" as a naturalized gospel/R&B number.[3]

Interpretive singers, then, tend to adhere fairly closely to the pitches established by composers when personalizing melodies, and in "Try a Little Tenderness," pitch deviation among the crooners runs from none at all in Bing Crosby's 1933 recording to the minor re-workings introduced by Crosby in 1955, Sinatra in 1946 and 1960, and Tormé in 1957. Example 2 samples the range of alterations these singers applied to the verses, the first part detailing the ways they treated the identical pitch structure of the first and fourth phrases and the second part presenting Sinatra's melodic contours for the third phrase (Crosby and Tormé did not deviate from the published sheet music in this last passage). Each version of the tune diverges somewhat from the sheet music, and in the first four cases shown in Example 2a (staves 2 to 5), the final three notes of the phrase remain unchanged, while the first and second notes are either raised or lowered (interestingly, on one occasion, both Sinatra and Tormé opt for the same pitch structure; see staff 2). In the last three staves, both sections of the tune undergo alteration, Frank Sinatra's 1960 melody straying the farthest from what the composers wrote, for although he begins and ends on their pitches, he varied the middle three notes (see staff 8). As this last passage demonstrates, Sinatra was slightly more adventurous in his modification of pitch the second time he recorded the song, and despite a great deal of consistency between the discs he made fourteen years apart (see, for instance, staves 3 and 4 of Example 2a), Example 2b further illustrates his later approach. On his 1946 recording, he adjusted only one note of the passage transcribed in the example (the second note in verse 2; see staff 2), but in 1960, he sang this phrase in the first verse as it was written and then deviated from the composers' pitches in the second and third verses, altering all five interior notes in the second verse (see staff 3) and changing the first and fourth notes in the third verse to produce a descending scale (see staff 4).

Example 2.   Pitch contour in "Try a Little Tenderness"

a   the first phrase of the verses

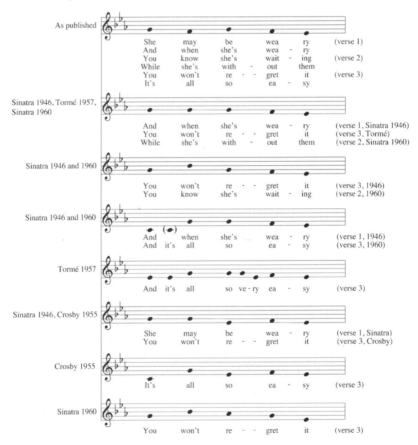

b   the third phrase of the verses

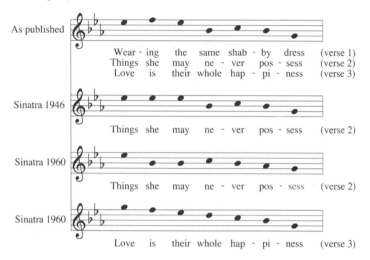

But beyond these minor deviations in pitch, the crooners liberally applied the "laws of prosody" to personalize the melodies they sang. In other words, they generated unique experiences for listeners by judiciously combining accent, emphasis, pausing, and syllable length with whatever pitch modifications they chose to introduce. This approach provided them with the tools they needed to align note values with the properties of normal speech so that their delivery would sound natural, or at least as natural as the crooning style would permit. Their general inclination was to lengthen vowels more than speakers would, and these longer vowels have certainly become one of the traits that distinguishes their performances from those of the younger generation of pop/rock/gospel/R&B singers. Yet despite their reliance on this manner of delivery, the crooners' interpretations still have the effect of liberating "Try a Little Tenderness" from the plain, four-square way it was notated in the published version, and Example 3 presents the rhythmic profile they imposed on the opening melody of the first verse, as well as the repetition of that tune in the fourth phrase of the stanza.

Example 3. Rhythmic profiles in the first verse of "Try a Little Tenderness"

a   first phrase

b   fourth phrase

The composers constructed the passages identically, setting the twin phrases, "she may be weary" and "and when she's weary," to the same rhythmically simple melody, and the singers elevated this music from its plainness by applying the principles of prosody differently in each section. The accents and emphases imposed on the first phrase allow the words and melody to come to life in four distinct patterns of stress (∪ = shorter/weaker, — = longer/stronger):

Crosby 1933/55	∪	∪	∪	—	∪
Etting 1933	∪	—	∪	—	∪
Sinatra 1946/60	—	∪	∪	∪	—
Tormé 1957	∪	∪	∪	∪	—
	She	may	be	wea-	ry

In both of his recordings, Bing Crosby treated the opening three words equally and then lightly ornamented the first syllable of "weary" not only to align his singing with the natural accentuation of the word (long-short) but also to make "weary" the focus of the phrase. Ruth Etting, on the other hand, in addition to giving "weary" its normal accentuation, emphasized the word "may" by placing it on the long note of a triplet figure. Sinatra also chose to emphasize one of the initial words, deciding to stress "she" in each of his recorded performances, and in 1946, he lengthened the second syllable of "weary" more than in 1960 to give the latter part of the word greater prominence. Tormé, like Sinatra had done in his recordings, reversed the normal accentuation of "weary," but in the first part of the phrase, he opted for Crosby's equal, non-emphatic treatment of the text.

This manner of organizing accent and emphasis uniquely defined the rhythmic character of the opening phrase for each singer, and in the fourth phrase, when the composers returned to the initial sentiment through similar words and an identical melody, the crooners enhanced the meaning of the text by subtly varying their prosodic delivery:

Crosby 1933	—	—	U	U	—
Etting 1933	—	—	U	U	U
Sinatra 1946	U	—	—	U	—
Crosby 1955	U	U	U	U	—
Tormé 1957	[omits]	—	—	U	—
Sinatra 1960	—	U	—	U	—
	And	when	she's	wea-	ry

Most of the singers decided not only to reverse the accentuation of "weary" but also to emphasize two of the opening words, the exceptions being Ruth Etting, who delivered the final word of the phrase as two short syllables, and Bing Crosby, who in 1955 chose to sing the first three words without emphasis. Of those opting for an emphatic approach, three of them, Crosby and Etting in 1933 and Sinatra in 1960, stressed the conjunction "and," a word that normally would not be emphasized in singing, or in speech for that matter, but would be uttered more like Sinatra did in 1946, as a short note leading to an emphatic word. Both Crosby and Etting decided to emphasize the following word "when," as well, and in 1960 Sinatra stressed "and" and then sang "when" in a non-emphatic way. Each of these approaches makes the fourth phrase distinct from the first, and collectively they demonstrate how the singers individualized the song simply by applying prosodic procedures to vary the tune's rhythmic structure.

In the bridge, the emotional climax of the song, even though most of the singers relied almost exclusively on prosodic delivery to generate interest, three of them introduced one minor structural change in the second phrase of the section. Crosby, Sinatra, and Tormé added an extra word to "she has her grief and care," and the inclusion of a second "her" just before the end of the line ("she has her grief and her care") required them to expand the melody accordingly (see Example 4). Initially, they all elected the same pitch amendment for "and her," but in 1960, Sinatra chose a stepwise melodic descent for the first three words of the phrase and then repeated that motion for the next three words.

Example 4. Bridge of "Try a Little Tenderness," second phrase

The crooners' adherence, for the most part, to the published pitches did not hinder their imaginative response to the text, however, for sensitive combinations of prosody and pauses enabled them to highlight specific words and the sentiments associated with them. For example, in the first line of the bridge, Etting and Sinatra (1946 and 1960) inserted a pause between "just" and "sentimental," and to borrow a concept from William Cockin (1775: 99), this had the effect of setting off and rendering more conspicuous the word "sentimental" (see Example 5). The vocalists also employed pauses to draw attention to other words and phrases, Etting placing stops before the expressions "and care" and "soft and gentle" to leave them impressed on the memory of the listeners with stronger effect, and Sinatra (1960) separating the words "soft" and "gentle" in order to bring them to notice (see Example 5). But beyond the effective use of space to reinforce the sentiments of the text, the crooners subtly vary the rhythmic profile of the melody to create patterns of accent and emphasis that further enhance the persuasiveness of their delivery.

Example 5.   Pauses in the bridge of "Try a Little Tenderness" (* = pauses of various lengths)

At ends of lines and within phrases	At ends of lines only
Crosby 1933	*Crosby 1955 & Tormé 1957*
It's not just sentimental *	It's not just sentimental *
She has her grief and care *	She has her grief and her care *
And a word * that's soft and gentle *	And a word that's soft and gentle *
Makes it easier to bear *	Makes it easier to bear *
Etting 1933	
It's not just * sentimental *	
She has her grief * and care *	
And a word that's * soft and gentle *	
Makes it easier to bear *	
Sinatra 1946	
It's not just * sentimental *	
She has her grief and her care *	
And a word that's soft and gentle *	
Makes it easier * to bear *	
Sinatra 1960	
It's not just * sentimental *	
She has her grief and her care *	
And a word * that's soft * and gentle *	
Makes it easier * to bear *	

These patterns fall into general shapes for each line of the bridge, and Example 6 illustrates the common placement of short and long notes across the first three phrases of the section. In the first line, all six singers more or less follow the basic outline shown in the example, but subtle rhythmic differences distinguish one performance from another (see Example 7). Each rhythmic profile brings that singer's delivery closer to normal speech, and while Crosby (1933) and Etting came the closest to the published score (even though Crosby introduced triplet figures and anticipated beats and Etting placed a pause after "just" and shortened the penultimate syllable of "sentimental"), the other singers personalized the tune to a greater extent. They shortened the value of the first note, Sinatra (1960) and Tormé metrically displacing the beginning of the phrase to a significant degree, and drew attention to "just" by assigning it a longer value. Similarly, their treatment of "sentimental" shows the diverse ways in which this group of singers organized the internal metrical structure of a multi-syllable word (see Example 7). In the remaining two lines shown in Example 6, several of the singers followed the general patterns indicated, but for each of these passages, two vocalists diverged significantly. Sinatra (1960) and Tormé, for instance, emphasized "she" in the second line of the bridge and then either delivered the middle five words of the phrase exclusively as short notes (Tormé) or placed stress on "grief" by assigning a somewhat longer value to it (Sinatra) (see Example 7). Analogously, both Crosby (1955) and Etting de-emphasized the word "soft" in the third strain through the shorter values they chose for the words "soft and gentle" (Etting) or "that's soft and gentle" (Crosby) (see Example 7).

Example 6. Basic patterns of long and short notes for each word in the first three lines of the bridge in "Try a Little Tenderness"

∪	∪	—	∪ ∪∪ —		
It's	not	just	sentimental		

∪	—	∪	—	∪	—
She	has	her	grief	and	care

∪	∪	—	∪	—	∪	∪ —
And	a	word	that's	soft	and	gentle

Example 7. Individualized melodies in the bridge of "Try a Little Tenderness"

All the crooners, then, ground their delivery in long-established principles of prosody and generate subtly nuanced vocal lines that not only
deviate somewhat from the pitches the composers wrote but also begin to
approach natural speech. In fact, the degree to which they personalized
"Try a Little Tenderness" determines where their performances might
be placed on the continuum mentioned earlier, a performance spectrum
which extends from a manner of singing that focuses on the delivery of
uninterrupted vocal lines as written by the composer (in other words,
the practices commonly found on the modern operatic stage) to a highly
articulated style of singing that has broken free from the confines of the
composer's pitches. The crooners might best be situated somewhere near
the midpoint of this continuum, for although they modified pitch to an
extent and came much closer to speech than opera singers, they were not
predisposed to embrace the type of highly articulated and pitch-varied

style that became the hallmark of the younger generation of singers who first came to prominence in the 1960s, particularly those from the gospel/soul/R&B tradition, such as Aretha Franklin and Otis Redding. Franklin and Redding, however, should not be set apart from the previous generation of singers completely, because despite occupying a position further along the continuum of articulation and pitch deviation than the crooners, their style was not formed in a vacuum. Indeed, they rooted their understanding of articulation in principles of prosody and felt free to alter the composer's pitches, even if at times these alterations re-created the tune.

Clearly, the approach taken by Franklin and Redding in "Try a Little Tenderness" conforms to a number of the performance traditions associated with the crooners, and in the opening phrase of the first verse, Franklin, after ornamenting the first note slightly, introduces the same pitch variant on the second note of the passage that Sinatra and Tormé had done (see Example 8a and compare it with Example 2a, staff 2). Redding similarly restricts his pitch alterations to the first two notes of the phrase, choosing to ornament the middle of the last three notes lightly, whereas Sam Cooke sings the pitches exactly as the composers wrote them (see Example 8a). But, of course, Cooke is much closer to the crooners' style than either of his soul/R&B contemporaries. Moreover, Franklin continues her performance with just one minor deviation in the second phrase of the verse (the fifth note of the passage), while Redding changes the pitch of the first three notes and then applies short appoggiaturas to the second part of the phrase (see Example 8b).[4] Not surprisingly, the alterations Cooke introduces in this passage do not differ significantly from those of the crooners (see Example 8b).

In addition to these similarities with the crooners, all three singers adhere to the basic rhythmic structure established by the composers, Cooke at one point even singing the same rhythms that Mel Tormé had done in 1957 (compare Cooke's interpretation of the passage shown in

Example 9a with that of Tormé in Example 3a, staff 6). But beyond this general feature of their performances, Franklin subdivides the slow quarter-note pulse of the song through triplets and, along with Redding, displaces the first and second phrases of the first verse (see Example 9).

Example 8. Pitch deviations introduced by Franklin, Cooke, and Redding in the first verse of "Try a Little Tenderness"

a   first phrase

b   second phrase

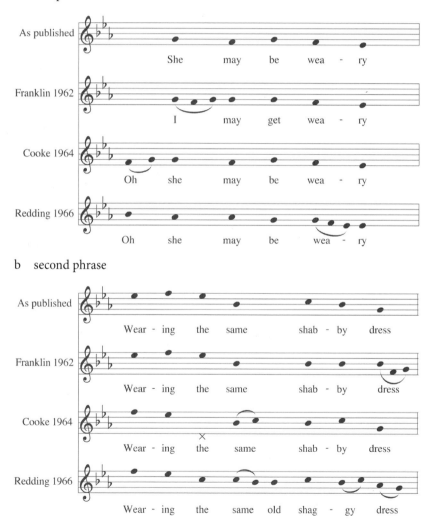

Example 9.   Rhythmic profiles of Franklin, Cooke, and Redding in the first verse of "Try a Little Tenderness"

a   first phrase

b   second phrase

Nonetheless, despite the parallels between the two groups of singers in the opening verse, both Franklin and Redding re-create the first two phrases of the bridge, Franklin personalizing the music primarily through ornamentation and word repetition and Redding turning the song "totally around" through significant pitch deviations, as well as ornamentation. Example 10 illustrates the type of interpolations Franklin favored. She adhered to the pitches the composers wrote for the first phrase but made the words more personal not only by changing them from "it's not just sentimental" to "I may be sentimental" but also by embedding the figure *epizeuxis* in the passage (the repetition of "I may be") and by drawing attention to the repeated words through a highly ornamented initial statement of "I may be" (see Example 10a). In the second phrase, she preserves the general contour of the composers' pitches while augmenting the line not with ornamentation but with ten new words that focus the sentiments on the singer herself (see Example 10b). Redding, on the other hand, radically deviates from the composers' pitches (except for the last note of the second phrase, which he extends by means of ornamental figuration), and in so doing reshapes the bridge, as he says himself, into a "brand new song" (see Example 10a, b). But quite apart from the pitch alterations Franklin and Redding introduce, they transform the section rhythmically and incorporate so many pauses that the bridge bears little resemblance to what the composers had conceived. Displacements of all sorts, as well as shorter note values and frequent stops, which set off words and ideas, allow the singers to individualize their rhythmic profiles to such an extent that "Try a Little Tenderness" emerges as a song which would not be out of place in the gospel/R&B tradition (see Examples 11 and 12).

Example 10.   Ornamentation and pitch deviation in the bridge of "Try a Little Tenderness"

a   first phrase

b   second phrase

Example 11. Rhythmic profiles in the bridge of "Try a Little Tenderness"

a   first phrase

b   second phrase

Example 12.   Pauses in the bridge of "Try a Little Tenderness"

Franklin 1962

Now I may be * I may be sentimental *

But I want to say * that I've had my griefs * oh and I've had my cares *

And just a good word * soft and gentle *

Makes it * makes it easier * easier to bear *

Redding 1966

It's not * just * sentimental no, no, no *

She has * her grief * and care yeah * yeah yeah *

But * the soft words * they are spoke so gentle yeah *

It makes it * easier * easier to bear *

These dramatic melodic alterations distinguish re-creative singers from those who prefer to interpret music within a much narrower range of parameters. Both types of singers clearly employ principles of prosody to shape their melodic lines, even though they differ significantly in the amount of pitch alteration and ornamentation they choose to incorporate in their performances. Nonetheless, prosodic delivery remains foundational to each style of singing, so much so that melodies in the world of 1960s pop/rock might better be referred to as prosodic tunes.

Chapter 3

Guitar-Based Modalities

During the 1960s, as the guitar became a pervasive force in popular music, harmonic practices emerged that were based more on the technical proficiency of self-taught guitarists than on traditional principles of harmony. The ease with which novices could master basic chords in first position (C, G, D, A, E, Am, Em, Dm, etc.) and simple barré formations (derived from first-position E, A, Em, and Am chords) determined the harmonic character of many songs from the decade. Indeed, songwriters began to feature sounds produced by first-position chords proceeding from C to A, F to D, and G to E, as well as the parallel motion of barré formations moving up and down the neck of the instrument.[1] Typical progressions from the mid and late 1960s range from those found in Tommy James and the Shondells' "I Think We're Alone Now," Donovan's "Hurdy Gurdy Man," and the Bee Gees' "Words" to those that were more obviously guitar oriented, such as Otis Redding's "(Sittin' on) the Dock of the Bay" and Bob Dylan's "Lay Lady Lay."[2]

Scholars interested in the harmonic structure of songs like these frequently apply concepts developed for classical music to pop/rock and tend to label chords with Roman numerals that designate a chord's function within a system of common-practice tonality.[3] Inevitably, when certain songs are placed in this theoretical framework, harmonic motion is seen as either deficient or non-traditional. Daniel Harrison (1997: 38–39), for example, finds The Beach Boys' "God Only Knows" to lack both "cadential drive" and a tonal center, especially since E and A compete for "tonic control" of the song, and in the refrain of "California Girls," Brian Wilson "thwarts" expectations because he does not allow the I — ii[7] progression of the first two chords (B C♯m7) to continue to V. Instead, he accesses remote keys through sequential repetition (A Bm7 G Am7) and, apparently, frustrates the listener's tonal proclivities in the process. But perhaps tonal expectations were never meant to exist in "California Girls," for the refrain simply may involve a pair of barré chords moving down by step in a scale that is neither major nor minor; that is, the harmonic style of the song may lie outside the confines of common-practice tonality.[4]

Moreover, when Ken Stephenson (2002: 116) applies tonal thinking to the chord structure of "(Sittin' on) the Dock of the Bay," he labels the chords in the following way and cites the song as an example of "non-traditional" secondary dominants:

G   B   C   A | G   E   G   E   G   A   G   E
I   V/vi IV V/V | I   V/ii I   V/ii I   V/V I   V/ii

In my view, however, he mistakenly presumes that the composers, Steve Cropper and Otis Redding, not only conceived the song within a tonal framework but also deliberately set out to exploit secondary dominants in an extraordinary way. Stephenson's circuitous labeling of the harmonic events seems to be predicated on the questionable notions that a G major scale (with its attendant fixed hierarchy of chord function) underpins the song and that any major chord appearing in the song, other than those built on the tonic (G), subdominant (C), or dominant (D), must act as a secondary dominant.[5]

Similarly, Walter Everett (2000a: 321) views the chords in "Lay Lady Lay" from a tonal perspective, and he describes the main chord progression in the song, A C♯m G Bm, which he labels I–"III"–♭VII–II[7],[6] as a "nonfunctional chord succession" acting in anticipation of the dominant (V) chord, a chord which first appears at the words "whatever colors you have in your mind" after six repetitions of the main progression. In other words, he assigns a tonal function to all chord progressions even when they deviate from the norms of functional tonality. A few sentences later, Everett concludes that there can be no harmonic motion without the presence of dominant harmony. He leads readers to this idea through Graham Nash's "Lady of the Island," where "the dominant is weakened to the point that the listener does not actually expect it to sound in this style, but it still haunts by its absence." Without V, songs like Dylan's "Girl from the North Country" make "no suggestion of harmonic motion at all; the repeated I–III–IV–I 'progression' constitutes a contrapuntal expansion of I with III acting like a modified I[6], and IV simply providing neighbors to I" (2000a: 321). According to Everett, then, strong harmonic motion cannot occur unless dominant harmony functions properly within a tonal realm. However, as Everett, Harrison, and Stephenson have also observed, much of the popular music from the 1960s routinely deviates from tonal expectations, and perhaps the time has come for us to recognize that this seemingly recalcitrant music actually employs harmonic principles different from those of common-practice tonality. Scholars who practice formalist analysis, particularly those who prize the application of Schenkerian techniques to popular music, have been slow to recognize the problems inherent in the imposition of one musical culture on another, even though fundamental misreadings of the music may result. Robert Walser (2003: 23) cautions that "[because] music can more easily be understood as interpretable within one's own discursive

competency[,] we often hear unfamiliar music systems as not having system at all, or as warped versions of the systems we know." Undoubtedly,
the chord progressions in popular songs need to be heard in a way that
is more closely aligned to the aural traditions of the musicians who created the music than to the habits of scholars steeped in the conventions
of common-practice tonality.[7]

The theoretical framework generated by these distinct harmonic
principles might well be described as a guitar-based modality, a system
that understands both scales and chord progressions from within the
idiomatic nature of guitar playing, as well as the processes of songwriting and recording.[8] When composing a song, guitarists normally create
just the basic framework, that is, chord progression and vocal line, and
during rehearsals or at the time of recording other musicians add parts
for bass, drums, lead guitar, and so on. Indeed, by the late 1960s the sonic
surface of a recording frequently was achieved through a cumulative
process in which guitar, bass, keyboard, vocal, and drums were recorded
independently. These additions often generated counterpoint within the
overall texture of a recording but they rarely altered the way recordists
thought about the basic chord progression of the song as conceived by the
songwriter. From within this stratified texture, then, I propose to isolate
the chord progression and place it in a theoretical system in which scales
are modal and each degree of a scale, being free from the type of hierar-
chical function prescribed by theories of common-practice tonality, may
have either a major or minor chord built on it (plus extensions, such as
6ths, 7ths, 9ths, etc.). These modes center harmonically on the first note
of the scale, and a strong sense of motion between chords occurs when
roots move by a second, third, fourth, or fifth, for this style does not rely
exclusively on root movement by a fifth to create powerful progressions.
Chords are identified by name (C, Am, D7, etc.), following not only the
standard parlance of popular musicians but also the normal practice of
published sheet music, and each mode is labeled traditionally (Dorian,

Phrygian, Lydian, Mixolydian, Aeolian, or Ionian). But this latter nomenclature does not imply that medieval, Renaissance, or jazz modal practices are present in popular music of the 1960s. The labels merely specify the interval pattern of an eight-note scale (see Example 1).

Example 1.   Modal scales

Dorian:	D E F G A B C D
Phrygian:	E F G A B C D E
Lydian:	F G A B C D E F
Mixolydian:	G A B C D E F G
Aeolian:	A B C D E F G A
Ionian:	C D E F G A B C

The system outlined above departs from the theoretical models normally applied in formalist studies of popular music, and it requires us to abandon notions of modal purity, especially when notes beyond the seven discrete pitches of a modal scale are featured in songs from the 1960s. For example, an A-major chord built on the second step of the Mixolydian scale introduces C♯ into the harmonic texture, a note many music theorists would consider foreign to the Mixolydian mode, but in the system I propose, this type of addition does not violate the integrity of the mode, for modal identity is determined by the scale upon which the chord progression is based and not by the major or minor color of the triads built on the steps of that scale. In other words, theories of alteration and modal subversion do not need to be invoked to explain the presence of major chords on scale degrees modal purists would deem inappropriate for such sonorities. Indeed, the cross-relations produced by notes that lie outside the scale (for example, the C/C♯ and G/G♯ conflicts embodied in the Mixolydian chord progressions C to A and G to E) have been a normal part of modal systems from at least the sixteenth century, and we probably should adjust our understanding of modality to reflect the flexible practices of musicians.[9]

In order to explore this method of harmonic organization, I will discuss five of the songs mentioned at the outset, all of which conform to the guitar-based modal style and topped the charts in either the UK or the USA: "(Sittin' on) the Dock of the Bay," "Lay Lady Lay," "I Think We're Alone Now," "Hurdy Gurdy Man," and "Words."[10] The first four songs demonstrate various procedures in the Mixolydian mode, and the fifth song, "Words," illustrates the harmonic palette that becomes available when the Mixolydian scale is transformed into G-Dorian by lowering B to B♭. In some of these songs, such as "(Sittin' on) the Dock of the Bay" and "Lay Lady Lay," chords are built on every step of the scale, but in other songs, such as, "I Think We're Alone Now," "Hurdy Gurdy Man," and "Words," one or more degrees have been omitted. All chords may be major, as in "(Sittin' on) the Dock of the Bay" and "Words," but commonly the chords employed in songs from the mid and late 1960s are a mixture of major and minor triads.

"(Sittin' on) the Dock of the Bay" exemplifies the close relationship between guitar technique and harmonic idiom, for Steve Cropper's signature riffs, staples of his style, provide the impetus for the harmonic direction of the chorus, bridge, and verse (the superstructure and chord progressions of the song are shown in Example 2). These riffs are built around major chords and not surprisingly a major chord occurs on every step of the scale:

d	e	f♯	g	a	b	c	d
b	c♯	d♯	e	f♯	g♯	a	b
G	A	B	C	D	E	F	G

Movement between these chords is usually by a second, third, or fourth, the precise motion being determined by the direction Cropper's riffs and figures take.

Example 2. Superstructure and chord progressions, "(Sittin' on) the Dock of the Bay" (normalized, as many of the chords anticipate the beginning of the bar by an eighth note)

Intro (4 bars)

G | G | G | G |

Verse 1 (8 bars)

||: G | B | C BB♭ | A :||

Chorus (8 bars)

G | E | G | E | G | A | G | E |

Verse 2 (8 bars)

||: G | B | C BB♭ | A :||

Chorus (8 bars)

G | E | G | E | G | A | G | E |

Bridge (8 bars)

G D | C | G D | C | G D | C | F | D |

Verse 3 (8 bars)

||: G | B | C BB♭ | A :||

Chorus (8 bars)

G | E | G | E | G | A | G | E |

Outro (8 bars whistling then to fade)

||: G | G | G | E :||

Cropper's most memorable riff, an important hook in the song, is, of course, featured prominently in the chorus, and he constructs this riff so that the G chord it embodies may progress to either E, A, or B. In the first half of the chorus, the riff takes the harmony from G to E, but in the second half, it leads to a new figure on A (see Example 3). In the verse, however, Cropper truncates the riff and proceeds directly to B through chromatic motion (see Example 4). The chords generated by this open-ended riff not only demonstrate the importance of root motion by seconds (G to A in bars 5–6 of Example 3) and thirds (G to E in bars 1–2 of Example 3), two strong harmonic progressions in music from the 1960s, but also reveal the non-functional nature of guitar-based modalities. The song clearly centers on G, and the motions to G from a third below (E to G in bars 2–3 of Example 3) and a second above (A to G in bars 4–5 of Example 4) help establish the focal point of the mode. In this style, nothing more is needed to create a powerful sense of harmonic motion to the center.

The bridge, like many bridges in songs from this era, provides harmonic and melodic relief, and Cropper diverges from the movement by thirds that dominated the verses and chorus with a popular guitar figure that requires the player to slide the interval of a sixth up or down by a step on adjacent pairs of strings (see Example 5). After three repetitions of the resulting chord progression (G D C [G]) and the pattern of harmonic motion it implies (↗5th, ↘2nd, ↘4th), the bridge closes with another strong progression common in the music from this era. Here, Cropper first descends in sixths from G to F and then moves up the fingerboard to a new figure built on a D chord before he returns to the modal center and the riff of the third verse. In isolation, the final progression from D to G might be considered by some to be tonal (dominant to tonic), but in a modal system, root movement by a fifth simply provides another way of proceeding to the center that is no more powerful than motion by a second, third, or fourth.[11] In fact, Cropper's main bridge figure illustrates how non-functional parallel motion of the type prevalent in guitar playing may be used to reinforce a modal center.

Example 3. Chorus riff, "(Sittin' on) the Dock of the Bay"

Example 4. Verse riff (taken from the third verse), "(Sittin' on) the Dock of
the Bay"

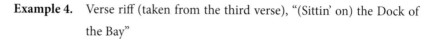

Example 5.   Bridge figure, "(Sittin' on) the Dock of the Bay"

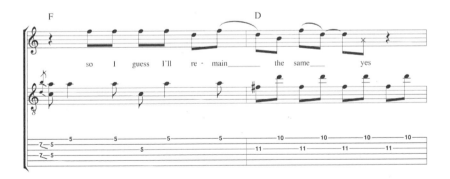

Bob Dylan's "Lay Lady Lay" further illustrates the ways in which guitar technique can influence harmonic design. The song is based on a Mixolydian scale transposed to A (see Example 6), and Dylan exploits barré formations moving down the neck of the instrument one fret at a time to create the pattern A C♯m G Bm, a harmonic unit that is repeated twenty times over the course of the song (the superstructure and chord progressions are shown in Example 7). In this progression, a pair of adjacent barré chords a third apart, one major and the other minor, descends by step to produce both a chromatic line and parallel motion (see Example 8). On each repetition of the pattern, Dylan returns to the modal center A from Bm. This stepwise descent certainly affirms the mode's focal point, and the recordists find other ways to reinforce the modal center as well. Throughout the recording, a pedal-steel guitar emphasizes the descending chromatic line outlined in the predominant harmonic unit, but in both the middle section of each verse and the bridge, the pedal-steel player reaffirms the modal center with a figure that embodies root motion by a fourth from D to A (see Example 9). The bass player, on the other hand, reinforces the focal point of the mode in a different manner. In order to mark the return of the main chord progression at several important structural moments, he slides from the pitch E up to the pitch A at the beginning of the first and second verses, as well as after the harmonic excursion (E F♯m A) in the middle of each verse (see Example 10). Undoubtedly, Dylan places this digression at the midpoint of the verses to provide relief from the repetitions of the main harmonic unit, and the motion from E through F♯m to A appears to shift the modal center to E. Indeed, the rising and falling fourths certainly seem to confirm E as the focal point, and in the last bar of the passage, the bass player's sliding figure has a double effect. It makes the final chord of the excursion sound as though it belongs to a progression centered on E while it establishes A as the modal center of the next section.

Example 6.   Scale and chords, "Lay Lady Lay"

e	f♯	g♯	a	b	c♯	d	e		
c♯	d	e	f♯	g♯	a	b	c♯		
A	B	C♯	D	E	F♯	G	A	⇒	A-Mixolydian

Example 7.   Superstructure and chord progressions, "Lay Lady Lay"

Intro (8 bars)

||: A | C♯m | G | Bm :||

Verse 1 (32 bars)

||: A | C♯m | G | Bm :|| 4x

||: E | F♯m | A | A :||

||: A | C♯m | G | Bm :||

Verse 2 (32 bars)

||: A | C♯m | G | Bm :|| 4x

||: E | F♯m | A | A :||

||: A | C♯m | G | Bm :||

Bridge (16 bars)

C♯m | C♯m | E A | A | C♯m | C♯m Bm | A | A |

C♯m | C♯m | E A | A | C♯m | C♯m | Bm | Bm |

Verse 3 (32 bars)

||: A | C♯m | G | Bm :|| 4x

||: E | F♯m | A | A :||

||: A | C♯m | G | Bm :||

Outro (5 bars)

A | Bm | C♯m | D | A ||

Example 8.   Main harmonic unit, "Lay Lady Lay"

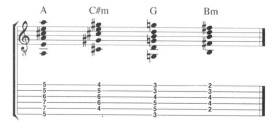

Example 9.   Pedal-steel guitar figure, "Lay Lady Lay"

Example 10.   Bass figure, "Lay Lady Lay"

Clearly, Bob Dylan derives his progressions from the guitar, and he combines barré and other hand positions to create patterns of major and minor chords that appeal to his musical sensibilities. He prominently features root motion by seconds (Bm A), thirds (A C#m, G Bm), and fourths (D A) in "Lay Lady Lay," and the indispensability of fourths to the modal style of the song is highlighted in the outro, where an ascending stepwise movement from A to D brings the song to its ultimate close through a falling fourth (A Bm C#m D A). The internal logic governing Dylan's guitar-based progressions, as well as those by Cropper and Redding in "(Sittin' on) the Dock of the Bay," informs much of the popular music from this decade, and Tommy James and the Shondells'

"I Think We're Alone Now" and Donovan's "Hurdy Gurdy Man" provide further examples of established practices in the modal style.

Both of these songs employ standard chord progressions of the era in a riff-like manner, "I Think We're Alone Now" highlighting root movement ↗5th, ↘2nd, ↘4th[12] and "Hurdy Gurdy Man" exploiting a progression that begins on the seventh step of the scale and descends by fourths to the modal center. "I Think We're Alone Now" is based on the Mixolydian scale transposed to A (see Example 11), and the track receives its sonic signature right at the outset with the bass and muted guitar announcing the main progression, A E D A, through root movement (see Example 12). This sonic signature returns frequently in the song, for it underpins the chorus, but in the verses, the harmony ascends by a third and then a fourth before it returns to the modal center by way of a falling fifth (A C♯m F♯m E [A]; the superstructure and chord progressions of the song are shown in Example 13). The pre-chorus, however, emphasizes the focal point of the mode differently. The first half alternates C♯m with A, and the second half employs one of the customary methods for approaching modal centers; that is, it descends from the seventh step of the scale to the fifth step and then proceeds to the focal point (G E A).

Example 11.   Scale and chords, "I Think We're Alone Now"

e		g♯	a	b	c♯	d	e		
c♯		e	f♯	g♯	a	b	c♯		
A	B	C♯	D	E	F♯	G	A	⇒	A-Mixolydian

Example 12.   Sonic signature, "I Think We're Alone Now"

bass and muted guitar

Example 13.   Superstructure and chord progressions, "I Think We're Alone Now"

Intro (4 bars)

A | E | D | A |

Verse 1 (8 bars)

‖: A | C♯m | F♯m | E :‖

Pre-Chorus (8 bars)

C♯m | A | C♯m | A |
G | G | E | E |

Chorus (8 bars + 2 bar extension)

‖: A | E | D | A :‖ A | A |

Verse 2 (8 bars)

‖: A | C♯m | F♯m | E :‖

Pre-Chorus (8 bars)

C♯m | A | C♯m | A |
G | G | E | E |

Chorus (8 bars + 2 bar extension)

‖: A | E | D | A :‖ A | A |

Outro (Chorus to fade)

‖: A | E | D | A :‖

The main chord riff in "Hurdy Gurdy Man" is constructed in a similar manner except that it descends by fourths to produce the progression F C G. Twenty-eight repetitions of this pattern dominate the song, the only relief occurring in the verses, where Donovan places the progression G Bm C D (the scale, superstructure, and chord progressions are shown in Examples 14 and 15). These two patterns, as well as the ones in "I Think We're Alone Now," represent standard but contrasting subsets of the harmonic palette available within the Mixolydian scale, and they illustrate the diversity of harmonic movement possible in a modal system. The descending progressions in "Hurdy Gurdy Man" (F C G) and "I Think We're Alone Now" (G E A) are unmistakably modal,[13] whereas the chords in the verses of the two songs, because they traverse the first, third, fourth, and fifth steps of the scale (G Bm C D—"Hurdy Gurdy Man") and the first, third, sixth and fifth steps (A C♯m F♯m E—"I Think We're Alone Now"), generate the type of harmonic motion that music theorists usually characterize as tonal. These motions are, however, a normal part of guitar-based modality, and they broaden our knowledge of the range of chord progressions songwriters consider viable in the Mixolydian mode. But when the third step of the Mixolydian scale (B) is lowered by a semitone to B♭ and the mode is transformed into G-Dorian, new patterns of harmonic organization emerge, especially in the way the modal center is approached.

Example 14.   Scale and chords, "Hurdy Gurdy Man"

d		f♯	g	a		c	d
b		d	e	f♯		a	b
G	A	B	C	D	E	F	G

Example 15.   Superstructure and chord progressions, "Hurdy Gurdy Man"

Intro (4 bars)

‖: F C | G :‖

Verse 1 (4 bars)

‖: G Bm | C D :‖

Pre-Chorus (4 bars + 1 bar extension)

‖: F C | G :‖ G |

Chorus (8 bars)

‖: F C | G :‖ 4x

Verse 2 (4 bars)

‖: G Bm | C D :‖

Pre-Chorus (4 bars + 1 bar extension)

‖: F C | G :‖ G |

Chorus (8 bars)

‖: F C | G :‖ 4x

Guitar Solo (16 bars)

‖: F C | G :‖ 8x

Outro (Chorus to fade)

‖: F C | G :‖ 5x, fades on 6th repetition

Songwriters, such as the Gibb brothers of the Bee Gees, certainly took advantage of the harmonic implications of the G-Dorian scale, for the main chord progression in their song "Words" relies on the B♭ of this scale for its effect (the scale, superstructure, and chord progressions are shown in Examples 16 and 17). In fact, the prominent display of B♭ in the verse, coupled with the use of major chords throughout the song, helps give the track its characteristic sound. After a four-bar introduction, the first half of the verse proceeds from G to A and then traverses the fifth (D) and fourth (C) steps of the scale, one of the customary paths to the modal center. At the end of this opening section, the intensity of the performance increases in preparation for the harmonic lift from G to B♭, and this level of energy does not subside until the focal point of the mode has been reached once again (in the thirteenth bar of the verse). The course of harmonic movement across this approach to the central chord (B♭ F G) underscores the importance not only of the falling fourth in these progressions but also of the dramatic effect produced by motion to the modal center from the step below. The second verse retains the harmonic pattern of the first, except that the B♭ chord proceeds directly to D instead of the seventh step of the scale. The ensuing chorus simply alternates between G and D, and just as in "Lay Lady Lay," the indispensability of fourths to the modal style is highlighted in the outro, where motion from C to G is outlined.

Example 16.   Scale and chords, "Words"

d	e	f	g	a		c	d		
b	c♯	d	e	f♯		a	b		
G	A	B♭	C	D	E	F	G	⇒	G-Dorian

Example 17.   Superstructure and chord progressions, "Words" (on the fifth step of the scale the guitarist plays D7, while the pianist plays D)

Intro (4 bars)

G | G | G | G |

Verse 1 (16 bars)

G | G | A | A | D | D | CG | G |

B♭ | B♭ | F | F | G | G | A | D |

Verse 2 (11 bars)

G | G | A | A | D | D | CG | G |

B♭ | B♭ | D |

Chorus (4 bars +1 bar extension)

[D] | G | D | G | D |

Verse 2 (11 bars; 1st 8 bars hummed)

G | G | A | A | D | D | CG | G |

B♭ | B♭ | D |

Chorus (12 bars)

‖: [D] | G | D | G :‖ 3x

Outro (3 bars)

C G | C G | C G ‖

The harmonic palette of popular music from the late 1960s undoubtedly owes much of its distinctive character to the musical habits of guitarists, for these musicians frequently exploit easily negotiable hand positions to produce riffs and chord progressions that comfortably fit their instrument. They freely place major chords on every step of the scale and often move between these chords in a way unique to the guitar. Root movements by seconds, thirds, fourths, and fifths are valued equally, and strong progressions are created through various means: descending motion (7–5–1, 7–4–1, 5–4–1, 4–1),[14] ascending/descending motion (4–5–1), as well as movement by ascending or descending seconds (7–1, 2–1) and thirds (6–1, 3–1). In fact, the flexibility of a guitar-based system of modality allows these progressions to be viewed more from the perspective of the guitarists who invented them than from a world of common-practice tonality foreign to most popular musicians.

Part II

THE RECORDED WORK

Chapter 4

Bel Canto:
The Unbroken Tradition

In transforming the basic structure of a song into effective musical discourse, recordists strive to heighten the impact of the lyrics, melody, and harmony through an emotionally persuasive performance designed to enhance the expressive flow of the narrative. The presentation of the song's story falls to the singer, and not surprisingly most Top 40 records from the 1960s focus the listener's attention on the vocal track. Singers reinforce the linear progression of emotional events embedded in the song through a manner of performance which draws upon the sorts of vocal techniques and interpretive strategies that have been available for centuries, and, as noted in Chapter 2, the style of singing captured on tape during the 1960s can bear a striking resemblance to *bel canto* procedures dating from the late eighteenth and early nineteenth centuries. Indeed, beyond the "laws of prosody," many other aspects of the vocal performances emanating from the grooves of pop/rock recordings comfortably map on to the verbal depictions and notated examples that survive from the earlier period.[1]

A finite range of vocal techniques helps singers tell their stories convincingly, and performers move listeners by utilizing the tools of expression at their disposal: emphasis, accent, tone of voice, register, phrasing (pauses and breathing), *legato, staccato, portamento, messa di voce,* tempo (particularly rhythmic *rubato*), *vibrato,* and ornamentation. The precise mix of features singers adopt defines their style of performance, and similarities of approach result from the decision, either conscious or unconscious, to maximize certain elements and minimize others. The ways in which these devices are realized, then, and the degree to which singers favor or disfavor a single component or cluster of components not only determines the collective fashion of an era or genre but also distinguishes individual habits within identifiable general customs.

Popular artists tend to prize many of the elements of expression that formed the basis of singing in the late eighteenth and early nineteenth centuries, and the differences that set apart the performance of pop songs in the 1960s from the lineages of European art music are much fewer than commonly thought.[2] In fact, the older *bel canto* tradition survives more in the world of pop and jazz singing than it does on today's operatic stages, even though classically-trained singers fervently believe they perform in a true *bel canto* way. Over the past hundred years, the *bel canto* style, as practiced in art music, has evolved to center almost exclusively on the production of "beautiful" tone and the exhibition of that tone through the uninterrupted delivery of long, heavily vibrated lines. But historically, the manner of singing embodied in the words *bel canto* embraced much more than *bel suono* (beautiful sound), for during the 1800s singers valued the entire range of techniques listed above. Hence, in the latter part of the nineteenth century the words *bel canto* ("beautiful singing"), and not *bel suono,* encapsulated the attributes of vocal style.[3]

This older tradition is certainly present in the modern world of pop/rock singing, and an examination of vocal tracks from the 1960s through this 200-year-old lens reveals the extent to which pop artists embrace *bel canto* techniques. Highly articulated phrasing, *messa di voce* (swell), prosodic accent, emphasis, rhythmic displacement (*tempo rubato*), gradations of *legato* and *staccato*, *portamento*, ornamentation (especially appoggiaturas), changes of register and tonal quality of the voice, as well as selectively introduced *vibrato*, all figure prominently in pop/rock recordings, and the first item from this list, highly articulated phrasing, provides a striking illustration of the differences between the modern classical approach and the pop style of the 1960s. The old *bel canto* singers, just like speakers of their day, made the sense of the sentences they uttered clear to listeners by incorporating grammatical and rhetorical pauses frequently, one writer from the eighteenth century suggesting as often as every fifth or sixth word (Robertson 1785: 75).[4] Grammatical pauses coincided with the location of notated punctuation (commas, colons, and full stops), and singers inserted rhetorical pauses in places where, although stops were not indicated, the sense of the sentences called for them. Pauses of varying lengths gave listeners an opportunity not only to reflect on what had just been said but also to anticipate what was to follow. In short, grammatical and rhetorical pauses allowed singers to convey a clear conception of the subject matter to the hearer in a natural manner akin to speaking. Obviously, this important technique of storytelling would be lost if singers delivered their melodies without inserting the types of stops listeners need to grasp the meaning of a text.

Led Zeppelin's "Stairway to Heaven" (1971) attests to the level of eloquence pop singers can achieve through the application of *bel canto* principles of articulation, and on the recording, Robert Plant employs both grammatical and rhetorical pauses to compartmentalize the ideas into easily discernable units. Most of the pauses help make the grammatical structure plainly evident, Plant placing stops of various lengths before prepositions (to, with, on, by, in, through, for), conjunctions (and, when, if, what, but, then), and relative pronouns (who), while dividing nominatives and objective completions from their verbs (see Example 1, lines 4 and 2 respectively). He also separates an expression in a direct address (line 7), as well as a preposed extension comprising a prepositional phrase (line 3), and pauses when a relative pronoun is understood (line 1). In addition, he sets off a parenthetical expression, one that may be omitted without injuring the construction (line 6), and introduces a rhetorical pause to separate an adjective from its noun (line 5). Normally, speakers and singers would never sever adjectives from their nouns, but the unexpected suspension of the voice Plant introduces between "new" and "day" interrupts the flow of the thought momentarily and draws attention to the sentiment expressed in a novel way.

Example 1.   Led Zeppelin, "Stairway to Heaven" (selected verses)
Single asterisks represent the shortest pauses introduced, double asterisks somewhat longer stops, and triple asterisks the longest pauses.

	Text	Type of pause
1	There's a lady who's sure ** all that glitters . . .	When relative pronoun "that" is understood
	. . .	
2	. . . sometimes words have * two meanings **	To separate objective completion from its verb
3	In a tree ** by the brook ** there's . . .	Before proposition; to separate preposed extension comprising a prepositional phrase
	. . .	
4	. . . all of our thoughts * are misgiven ***	To separate nominative from verb
	. . .	
5	. . . a new * day will dawn **	Rhetorical pause separating an adjective from its noun
	. . .	

Text	Type of pause
6 ... it won't go * (in case you don't know) **	To separate a parenthetical thought
...	
7 Dear lady * can you hear ...	To separate expression in a direct address

Speakers and singers use pauses, then, as William Cockin suggested in 1775 (p. 99), to render the sense of sentences more conspicuous, and the frequent insertion of stops created variety in their delivery. But the suppression of pauses could also enhance the effectiveness of sentences, especially if a singer wished to interpret a text differently on its repetition. Karen Carpenter, for example, in her cover of Lennon and McCartney's "Ticket to Ride," changed her conception of the first verse when it was repeated later in the song (see Example 2). On the original recording, John Lennon had sung the opening lines plainly, with just one articulation in the middle, but Carpenter recognized other places where pauses could be inserted. Singers often separate verbs from their complements, and an equally natural delivery may be achieved if stops are introduced after "think" in the first segment and "it's" in the second. Carpenter, however, initially chose to suppress the pause after "think," even though she momentarily suspended her voice between "it's" and "today," but on her repetition of the lines, she incorporated both stops. This subtle modification of her delivery emphasizes the words before and after the

Example 2. "Ticket to Ride"

John Lennon	Karen Carpenter	
0:07 I think I'm gonna be sad *	0:35	I think I'm gonna be sad *
I think it's today yeah		I think it's * today yeah
	2:33	I think * I'm gonna be sad *
		I think it's * today yeah

pause so that the ideas in the text are set off and rendered conspicuous in a much more arresting way.

Whenever singers articulate texts with these types of pauses, they create short melodic fragments that might sound disjointed if they were not entered and exited gracefully. In the *bel canto* era, performers allowed the voice to rise and fall with the idea expressed, and in 1833, John Turner remarked: "the greatest force and expression should be given to the middle of the phrase; the notes at the beginning and end being sung in a softer strain, and those at the end, in particular, never quitted abruptly, but gradually sunk, as it were, into silence" (p. 95). Domenico Corri (1810: 52, 65), writing earlier in the century, provided further details on the way singers should conclude phrases: "on the last note of a passage [that is, at any place where a singer finds it necessary to take breath], always die the Voice, and at each note of the final phrase, end thus <> this swell must be done as gentle as possible, only as much as to accent the sound, and immediately die it away." The technique of "dying the voice" was the equivalent of cadence in speaking (that is, the equivalent of speakers letting their voices fall at the stops indicated by punctuation), and singers avoided abrupt phrase endings not only by gradually sinking notes into silence but also by lightly and instantaneously quitting the final note of the passage, as Manuel García had recommended in the middle of the nineteenth century.[5] García maintained that if the final note of "figures, members of phrases, phrases, periods, and pieces . . . were . . . to be too much prolonged the thought would cease to be distinct and elegant; besides which, the prolongation of these final notes would make the singing heavy and would absorb part of the time necessary for renewing the breath." He then added "the note which ends a final period . . . should be longer than all the other final notes; because it marks the completion of a thought or discourse."

These principles form the basis of phrasing in popular singing, as well, and many performers let their dynamic shading rise and fall with the idea expressed, particularly when melodic lines trace an arc, whether in short phrases, such as occur in The Zombies' "Time of the Season" and The Righteous Brothers' "You've Lost that Lovin' Feelin'," or in longer phrases, such as those found in The Monkees' "Pleasant Valley Sunday" (see Example 3a, b). In other types of melodic structures, singers taper the phrase toward the end, thus creating the equivalent of the speaker's cadence, and they regularly conclude passages either with short notes or a dying voice reminiscent of the style Domenico Corri had described. Tom Jones, for example, often phrases in a cadential manner (see Example 3c), and Jimi Hendrix frequently employs short final notes in his cadences (see Example 3d). But other singers do not abbreviate final notes significantly, and in the Walker Brothers recording of Bacharach and David's "Make It Easy on Yourself," the last note of each sub-phrase remains lengthy even though it dies away (see Example 3e). Nonetheless, singers routinely shorten the ultimate notes of every line in a verse, as Mickey Dolenz did in the first verse of "I'm a Believer" (see Example 3f), and from time to time their approach to phrasing parallels García's suggestion that the last note of a larger section should be held longer than all the other final notes. Bob Dylan, for instance, adheres to this principle in "Positively 4th Street," where the ends of internal phrases are sung as short notes while the completion of thoughts are marked by extended values (see Example 3g). Similarly, Karen Carpenter reserves the longest note in "(They Long to Be) Close to You" for the ultimate word, and in addition to extending the note length, she incorporates a swell with *vibrato* added at the peak (see Example 3h), one of the common applications of vibration. She also introduces a swell on the final note of the first verse, but at this point in the song, her dynamic shading takes the form of a gentle accent, immediately died away, an approach similar to the one Domenico Corri had suggested for the final note of a phrase (see Example 3h).

Example 3.   Phrasing

a   The Zombies, "Time of the Season"

    0:08   It's the time * of the season

    The Righteous Brothers, "You've Lost that Lovin' Feelin'"

    0:10   And there's no tenderness * like before in your

            fingertips

b   The Monkees, "Pleasant Valley Sunday"

    0:09   The local rock group down the street is tryin' hard to learn

            their song

c   Tom Jones, "It's Not Unusual"

    0:45   If you should ever want to be loved by anyone

d   Jimi Hendrix, "Hey Joe"

    0:09   Hey Joe * where you going with that gun in your

            hand

e   Walker Brothers, "Make It Easy on Yourself"

    0:12   Oh * breaking up * is so * very hard to do

f   The Monkees, "I'm a Believer"

    0:05   I thought . . . tales

            Meant for . . . me

            Ah love . . . me

            That's . . . seemed

            Disappointment . . . dreams

g   Bob Dylan, "Positively 4th Street"

    1:54   You see me on the street

            You always act surprised

You say, "How are you?" "Good luck"

But you don't mean it

h   Carpenters, "Close to You"

    0:27   Close to you

    2:49   Close to you

A number of authors considered the swell, or *messa di voce*, as it was also known in the late eighteenth and early nineteenth centuries, to be the principal source of expression, and the technique of commencing a note softly, gradually augmenting its loudness to the middle, and then diminishing it insensibly to the end originated in the natural delivery of the spoken word. Thomas Philipps, writing in 1826, pointed out the close connection between speaking and singing in this regard:

> The *action* of increasing and diminishing on EVERY NOTE in singing, will be found, on examination, to arise from the NATURAL SPEAKING DELIVERY OF WORDS; which delivery would prove dissonant to the ear, if the sustained syllables, either on the vowel-sounds, or those of the liquid consonants, were to be given with EQUAL STRENGTH, instead of a SWELL and DECREASE, or as PARALLEL LINES would express = instead of the RHOMBOID <>. IN SINGING, it will be found of advantage to establish this mode of delivery by rules and practice: IN SPEAKING, we employ it without being aware that we do so; but observation will make evident, that from this *action* of the voice proceeds the melody of the SPEAKER; and the SINGER'S NOTES, though possessing power, tone, and compass, WILL BE HARSH, and UNMELODIOUS, IF DELIVERED WITHOUT the CRESCENDO and DIMINUENDO. (p. 5)

Although commonly applied to individual notes, *messa di voce* could also be spread over several notes, particularly when they fall by step (see

Example 4a), and popular singers employ the swell in various ways. Jimi Hendrix, for instance, accents the ends of sub-phrases with it in "The Wind Cries Mary," when the final musical gesture involves two notes falling by step (see Example 4b), and Karen Carpenter applies *messa di voce* flexibly across phrases to produce a gentle undulating effect (see Example 4c).

Example 4.   *Messa di voce*

a   Handel, "Holy Lord God Almighty" (Nathan 1836: 187)

b   Jimi Hendrix, "The Wind Cries Mary"

                <>   <>   <>
    0:19   And the clowns * have all * gone to bed *

c   Carpenters, "We've Only Just Begun"

    1:39   Before the risin' sun we fly

           So many roads to choose

Musical accents of this sort save performers from singing monotonously, and as demonstrated in Chapter 2, singers normally align these stresses with the prosodic implications of the text. In other words, vocalists impart life and interest to the melodies they sing by highlighting syllables and words in the same natural manner of speakers. Pop singers of all types generally deliver their texts prosodically, organizing their accents and emphases in the proper places to achieve a union of sense and sound, and Herb Alpert heightens the effect of Bacharach and David's "This Guy's in Love with You" through a judicious combination of natural sounding stresses and varied note lengths that help him establish the meaning he wishes to communicate (see Example 5a). Similarly, in "Magic Moments," Perry Como derives his accentuation of the first two words from speech (strong, weak; long, short) and provides contrast to this prosodic opening by equally stressing the syllables that follow (see Example 5b). He then draws the thought to a close with a cadence that parallels the structure of the final word (strong, weak). In the same vein, Dusty Springfield contrasts prosodically delivered words with non-prosodic singing to differentiate one phrase from another in "Wishin' and Hopin'" (see Example 5c). Here, the speech-like accentuation of the double-syllable words in the first line gives way to the equally stressed treatment of words in the second part of the passage, particularly "kisses" and "into."

Example 5.   Accent and emphasis (in the examples, ◡ represents less stress and — more stress)

a   Herb Alpert, "This Guy's in Love with You"

— — ◡ — ◡ —

2:38   Tell me now is it so

— — — — ◡ — ◡ —

Don't let me be the last to know

— — ◡ — ◡

My hands are shakin'

◡ — ◡ — — — ◡

Don't let my heart keep breakin'

— ◡ — ◡ —

Cause I need your love

◡ — ◡ —

I want your love

b   Perry Como, "Magic Moments"

— ◡ — ◡ — — — — — ◡

0:09   Magic moments when two hearts are caring

c   Dusty Springfield, "Wishin' and Hopin'"

— — ◡ — — ◡ — — ◡

1:02   Just wishin' and hopin' and thinkin'

. . .

— — — ◡ —

His kisses will start

— — — — — ◡ —

That won't get you into his heart

In these examples, the application of the principles of prosody to sing-ing required the performers to incorporate various gradations of light and shade in their vocal lines through *staccato*, a technique regularly employed beyond prosody to articulate the text in a natural manner. *Staccato* refers to a detached style of delivery which encompasses various degrees of brevity ranging from notes struck short in a pointed way to those made distinct through minimal detachment.[6] Writers in the nineteenth cen-tury suggested that singers execute the latter with gentle aspirations of the breast or impulses of the lungs so that a certain amount of stress is placed on each note in order to differentiate it more by emphasis than by detachment, a technique Manuel García (1857: 11) called *martellato*.[7] The opposite style of delivery, *legato*, calls for a flowing manner of singing in which performers smoothly connect individual notes with no break in sound. In the course of delivering vocal lines, singers routinely weave the two approaches together, as Dusty Springfield does in "The Look of Love." She alternates *legato* style with various degrees of detached vocalization in the first five lines of Example 6a, and then sings the remainder of the section in a smoothly flowing manner. Herb Alpert, on the other hand, in his recording of "This Guy's in Love with You," adopts an exclusively *staccato* approach throughout the passage shown in Example 6b, both pulsing on notes without abbreviating them, in a manner akin to García's *martellato*, and detaching notes with differing amounts of separation.

Example 6.   Gradations of *legato* and *staccato*

    a   Dusty Springfield, "The Look of Love"

        0:19   The look of love

                It's saying so much more

                Than just words could ever say

                And what my heart has heard

                Well it takes my breath away

                I can hardly wait to hold you

                Feel my arms around you

                How long I have waited

                Waited just to love you

                Now that I have found you

                You've got the look of love

    b   Herb Alpert, "This Guy's in Love with You"

        0:58   I've heard some talk

                They say you think I'm fine

(*continued*)

Example 6.   (*cont.*)

Yes I'm in love

And what I'd do to make you mine

Tell me now is it so

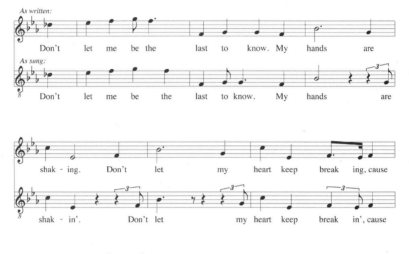

I need your love

I want your love

Some of these short notes are displaced rhythmically from their positions in Burt Bacharach's carefully notated score,[8] and this aligns Alpert with the old *bel canto* practice of altering notated rhythm through the application of *tempo rubato*, a performance technique which enabled singers to correct false accentuation and improperly set syllabic quantity (Bacon 1824: 84–85). *Tempo rubato* literally means stolen time, and writers from the early nineteenth century refer to borrowing time from or adding it to a note. At the singer's discretion, notes in the score may be lengthened or shortened so long as the time is restored within either the bar or the phrase, and the rhythms Bacharach had prescribed for "This Guy's in Love with You" would have given the text, to borrow Manuel García's words, "too regular and stiff a character" (1857: 50). Alpert's prosodic style of delivery, then, gracefully liberated the music from its inexpressive notation. Specifically, he remedied an inappropriately emphasized article, the word "the" in the first phrase of the music portion of Example 6b, and approximated spoken discourse by shortening and displacing the notes Bacharach had written for several words ("to," "are," "don't," and "my").

In their discussions of the *legato-staccato* complex, some writers in the early nineteenth century mention the gliding nature of smooth singing, and one of the techniques historically associated with the concept of *legato* carried its own designation. The term *portamento* represented a style of singing in which two distant notes were connected by indistinctly gliding or sliding through the intervening pitches in such a rapid way that these intermediate sounds were heard but not distinguished.[9] Singers matched their delivery of these gliding progressions to the sentiment of the text and varied the forcefulness of the slide accordingly, sometimes voicing it energetically and sometimes gracefully. Teachers of singing active at the time cautioned students to employ the technique sparingly lest the melody become nauseously languid and monotonous, and modern pop/rock practices seem to be aligned with this advice. Singers often use *portamento* just once in a passage to connect specific words with a slide that is either more or less pronounced. Perry Como, for example, applies the device in an obvious way to the first word of a phrase (see Example 7a), while The 5th Dimension displays the sounds within the glide quite prominently in the middle of a phrase (see Example 7b). Dionne Warwick, on the other hand, delicately joins words together at both the beginnings and ends of phrases through soft slides that at times are barely perceptible (see Example 7c).

Example 7. *Portamento*

    a   Perry Como, "Magic Moments"

          1:57   These ↘ magic moments filled with love

b   The 5th Dimension, "One Less Bell to Answer"
    1:30   Cause I still ↘ love him so

c   Dionne Warwick, "I'll Never Fall in Love Again"
    0:35   What do you get when you kiss a guy
            You get enough germs to catch pneumonia ↘
            After you do he'll never phone ya
            I'll never fall in love again
    1:43   I'm ↘ out of those chains, those chains that bind you
            That is why I'm here to remind you

The subtle nature of the *bel canto* style includes other imperceptible devices, as well, and singers regularly deliver individual words with appoggiaturas that leap to the main notes so quickly that they are scarcely discernible. Harriet Wainewright, writing in 1836, described this type of subsidiary leaning note as an imperceptible one that may proceed by step or leap (pp. 30–32). These quick appoggiaturas abound in the modern world of pop/rock singing, so much so that they could easily be regarded as a foundational component of the style. Some singers incorporated them at the end of virtually every phrase, B. J. Thomas, for instance, choosing to apply ascending motion to "Raindrops Keep Fallin' on My Head" and The Dave Clark Five favoring descending movement in "Do You Love Me" (see Example 8a, b). But singers used their knowledge of appoggiaturas to reinforce the structure of a song in other ways as well, especially when call-and-response passages were present. At the opening of "Do You Love Me," for example, the lead vocalist employed descending appoggiaturas at the ends of his lines while the backup singers responded with ascending motion (see Example 8c). Further variety could be achieved if singers chose to include both single and double appoggiaturas in their performances, and in Example 8d, The Buckinghams drew the first phrase to a close with a rapidly descending double appoggiatura and then applied somewhat longer single appoggiaturas, either ascending or descending by step, to the ends of the next three lines. David Clayton-Thomas, on the other hand, graced the passages from "Hi-De-Ho That Old Sweet Roll" shown in Example 8e exclusively with ascending appoggiaturas but varied the duration of the ornamental notes to make his delivery more persuasive. Initially, he added a long leaning note to the end of the first line and then applied an imperceptible appoggiatura to the last word of the section. But later in the song, when the words repeat, he did the reverse; that is, he employed an imperceptible appoggiatura at the beginning and saved his longest ornament for the final word, a moment of tension not released until he slides up to the note of resolution through *portamento* (see Example 8e).

Example 8. Appoggiaturas

a   B. J. Thomas, "Raindrops Keep Fallin' on My Head"

    0:04   Raindrops . . . on my head ↗

         . . . too big for his bed ↗

         Nothin' seems to fit ↗

b   The Dave Clark Five, "Do You Love Me"

    0:23   (Work it out ↘)

         I said work it out baby ↘

         (Work it out ↘)

         Ah you're driving me crazy ↘

         (Work it out ↘)

         A-with a little bit of soul now ↘

c   The Dave Clark Five, "Do You Love Me"

    0:02   Do you love me? ↘

(I can really move ↗)

Do you love me? ↘

(I'm in the groove ↗)

Do you love me? ↘

(Do you love me?) [no appoggiatura on the last word]

d   The Buckinghams, "Kind of a Drag"

↘ (cba)

0:44   Kind of a drag

↗ (ab)

When your baby says goodbye . . .

e   Blood, Sweat & Tears, "Hi-De-Ho That Old Sweet Roll"

↗ (b♭c) long

0:22   Gonna get me a piece of the sky

. . .

↗ (b♭c)

imperceptible

I'm singing hi-de-hi-de-hi-de-hi-de-ho

↗ (b♭c) imperceptible

1:15   I'm gonna get me a piece of the sky

. . .

↗ (b♭c) extended,

plus *portamento*

I'm singing hi-de-hi-de-hi-de-hi-de-ho

The techniques described here have formed the basis of expressive singing since the late eighteenth and early nineteenth centuries, and yet without an appropriate tonal quality of the voice to carry these devices to the ears of listeners, singers would be unable to deliver texts convincingly. In fact, singers in the first half of the nineteenth century were advised to vary the tonal coloring of their voices in order to avoid sounding monotonous, Mary Novello recommending in 1856 that young singers gain complete mastery over different and opposite qualities of tone (p. 15). The range of colors singers employed extended from those that were sweet and clear to those that were harsh and rough, and these qualities were further conditioned by the registral nature of the voice, for the registers themselves exhibited distinct tonal properties.

Register may be defined as a series of notes possessing a uniform character and quality of tone, and traditionally the human voice has been divided into two main registers, the chest and head voices.[10] The chest voice furnishes the lower notes of a singer's range and is full and sonorous, whereas the head voice, with its soft and light character, provides those notes lying above the chest range. And because these registers have distinct colors, classically trained singers usually blend them at the break so that when they pass from one to the other the notes surrounding the break are sung with a more uniform tone. Nonetheless, despite current classical practices, singers in both the *bel canto* and modern pop eras often use the head voice throughout their compass[11] and provide the tonal variety listeners expect by altering the color of the sounds they produce.

Pop singers regularly exploit strongly opposing tonal qualities and contrast soft, almost breathy, sounds with harder more metallic colors. In the passage shown in Example 9a, Sandie Shaw begins gently with a light subdued quality and progresses to a clear brilliant sound in the second half of the excerpt. Similarly, in "Both Sides, Now," Joni Mitchell contrasts delicate high notes, reminiscent of the "silken sort of under-voice" singers in the nineteenth century used in the "higher part of the scale,"[12] with tell. This includes, of course, the basic sound of the voice that, 200 years ago, appears to have contained little or no *vibrato*. Singers were expected to sing without any hint of trembling or wavering and those who could not were subjected to ridicule in the musical press, for as William Breare suggested in 1904 singers who become addicted to *vibrato* are unable to vary expression (p. 84, 91).[13] When applied selectively, *vibrato* could certainly heighten the impact of specific words and grace longer notes, just as Karen Carpenter did on the final note of "Close to You" (see Example 3h), but the continuously vibrated voice caused music to lose all feeling of rhythm, proportion, contrast, and most importantly, emotional significance. Performers, then and now, avoid the sort of tedium produced by the overuse of *vibrato* not only by incorporating a wide range of interpretive strategies in their delivery but also by applying the devices available to them in a variety of ways.

The principles of this expressive, re-creative style of singing have remained relatively constant for the past 200 years, and this unbroken tradition offers a means of bridging the gap between two seemingly disparate musical cultures. In fact, at least in certain regards, the practices of pop/ rock artists from the 1960s provide a fascinating model for performing late eighteenth- and early nineteenth-century art music in a way that seems to correspond more closely with historical documents than the literal, homogeneous approach taken by today's "classically" trained singers.

Chapter 5

Invention and Arrangement

Many songs begin their life in the imaginations of individual songwriters, and through the collaborative approach employed in recording popular music these songs are often transformed in the studio.[1] The creative process which brings about this transformation leads to the establishment of the sonic surface of a recording, and the rhetorical concepts of invention and arrangement furnish particularly helpful ways of thinking about that process as it unfolds from the initial conception of a song to the final mix captured on disc. In fact, the invention and arrangement of the subject matter of a discourse, as described in treatises on rhetoric, finds direct parallels in the compositional methods of songwriters such as Randy Bachman and Burton Cummings, both members of The Guess Who during the 1960s (Bachman, lead guitarist, and Cummings, lead singer and keyboard player). In his recent autobiography, co-written with John Einarson, Bachman speaks of an approach to songwriting that in certain respects is identical to the art of rhetoric. Bachman liked to analyze songs he heard on AM radio in order to discover what made them hits, and this enabled him to find the basic subject matter for musical discourse in the recordings of other groups, as well as in his own imagination. For example, The Guess Who's song "Laughing" (1969), written by Bachman and Cummings, drew some of its material from the Bee Gees' "New York Mining Disaster 1941" (1967), The Dave Clark Five's "Because" (1964a), and The Platters' "Twilight Time" (1958).[2] Bachman and Cummings identified and extracted a salient musical feature from each of these songs and adapted the borrowed material to create the opening, main chord progression, and one of the background vocals of "Laughing." The remaining "subject matter" of the song appears to have been the product of their own imaginations.

The technique of assembling a musical discourse from disparate sources mirrors the creative process in classical rhetoric, and in this chapter I discuss two elements of creativity, invention and arrangement, that are central to both rhetoric and songwriting/recording. In deriving the terminological and ideological basis for this discussion from the areas of rhetoric that deal with the finding of ideas and the arranging of those ideas in an artwork, I focus attention on the transformation of musical material. However, my interests in this chapter lie not in the technical details of making records or in the activities of recordists in their entirety, but in the ways songwriters and recordists discover and structure musical ideas, whether these activities occur in a collaborative way in a recording studio or in the private workspaces of individuals. In a sense, the discussion centers on form, but not form divorced from content, rather the creation of form from content.

Traditionally, rhetoric has been defined as the art of persuasive speech,[3] and the term invention refers to the discovery of ideas about the subject of a discourse through the systematic gathering of true or plausible matter that would make the case being presented convincing.[4] Orators sought material in existing concepts, judgments, and arguments and adapted it to the case at hand; that is, they collected ideas about the subject and analyzed them for their suitability. In order to discover "plentiful matter," to borrow Thomas Wilson's words written centuries ago, speakers mentally visited sets of prescribed topics (1533: 31–32). These topics were regarded as the seats or places, that is, the *loci*, of effective arguments and included universal topics, which contained arguments from time, analogy, opposition, cause and effect, definition, comparison, and so on, as well as special topics, which held arguments appropriate only for particular subject areas (for example, law or war).[5] Topics played an important role in invention, for they provided a formalized method of textual development and helped orators amass the best available materials, wherever they might be located. Once the arguments had been found, the orator marshaled the material in an order that would be the most persuasive and arranged the ideas according to their degree of conspicuousness (Ramée 1555: 145).[6] On a global level, the oration as a whole could be divided into as many as six large sections (introduction, statement of facts, division, proof, refutation, and conclusion) (*Rhetorica ad Herennium* 1954, III: ix, 16), whereas individual arguments often consisted of five components (proposition, reason, proof of the reason, embellishment, and résumé) (ibid., II: xviii, 28).

But orators could apply the principles of invention and arrangement in a masterful way only if their understanding of rhetorical methodology rested on the solid foundation of an education in a wide variety of subjects (Corbett 1990: 95). They acquired this liberal knowledge through reading, observation, and reflection and stored large reservoirs of potential material in their memories, a process similar to the one Randy Bachman describes for writing songs. Bachman enjoyed many different styles of popular music and had, in his own words, "a pretty wide palette" on which to draw (Einarson and Bachman 2000: 229). He and other composers, such as his co-writer Burton Cummings, assembled this varied palette by visiting *loci* pertinent to their activities; that is, they

major chord triad, and placed that before a Dave Clark Five chord pattern from *Because*, which was a well-worn pattern in dozens of songs
dating back to Irving Berlin. We [presumably Bachman and Cummings]
then took the background vocals from the Platters' *Twilight Time*, the
ascending "ahs," and put them in behind the lyrics. We did all this on
the spot. That was enough to get us started; the rest was original, the
idea of laughing at someone who broke your heart. (ibid.)

This description allows us to position the method of songwriting
adopted by Bachman and Cummings within the larger context of rhetorical construction, for Bachman not only informs us of the *loci* for three
of the important musical ideas used in the song but also reveals how the
discoveries were adapted and arranged. The A-minor chord which opens
the Bee Gees' "New York Mining Disaster 1941" (0:00–0:05) is played
in the fifth position on the guitar with a quick strumming motion (see
Example 1a), and in adapting this musical figure, Bachman converts the
minor triad to a major one and spaces out the arpeggiations (0:00–0:05;
see Example 1b). Instead of strumming the chord on every beat of the bar,
as the Bee Gees had done, Bachman arpeggiates it once at the beginning
of the bar and then repeats the top note of the chord on the remaining
three beats. The main harmonic argument of "Laughing" was found in a
chord progression that had become one of the commonplaces of popular
music, a static major harmony with a chromatic line running through it.
The specific *locus* which held this harmonic figure was The Dave Clark
Five hit, "Because." From this song, Bachman and Cummings selected
the first four bars of the verse harmony (0:08–0:16), transposed the
progression from G to A, and extended the chromatic line so that it not
only rose from E to G but also descended back to E (see Example 2). In
the penultimate two bars of the argument (0:18–0:23), they added D as a
bass note below the A harmony, before closing the progression on C♯m7
(0:24). As a means of reinforcing the tension created by the chromatic

motion, Bachman and Cummings placed a technique The Platters had used for the background vocals in "Twilight Time" behind one portion of the lyrics, that is, the idea of singing an accompanying line to "oo" or "ah" (see, for example, 0:03–0:20 in "Twilight Time").

Example 1.   Introduction, "Laughing"

a   "New York Mining Disaster 1941"

b   "Laughing"

Example 2.   Main harmonic argument, "Laughing"

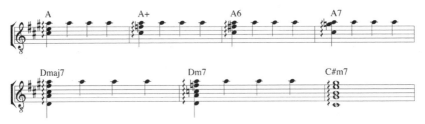

But suitable ideas, once found, needed to be fashioned into effective musical discourse, and Bachman's description reveals just how attentive the recordists were to arrangement. On a global level, the structural divisions in "Laughing" adhere to the pattern of an intro followed by verses alternating with a pre-chorus and chorus, and within each of these divisions, the discoveries were arranged and then enriched through the application of other musical figures. Bachman and Cummings certainly marshaled their material according to its conspicuousness, for they placed the idea with which they were most enthralled at the beginning. Functioning as an *exordium*, the arpeggiated A-major chord is designed to capture the listener's attention,[7] and like its counterpart in "New York Mining Disaster 1941," it provides the rhythmic impetus for the chord progression Bachman and Cummings selected to underpin the verses. Above this progression, the story begins to unfold, "I should laugh but I cry" (see Example 3), and the persuasiveness of Burton Cummings' singing has been enhanced by the way the components in the musical backdrop have been disposed. This type of arrangement, the distribution of ideas and instruments within the mix, allows recordists to manipulate the texture of songs in order to strengthen the overall effect of the final product. In "Laughing," each structural division, verse, pre-chorus, and chorus, has its own distinctive organization, and the three divisions, taken as a whole, have been arranged to lead the listener up a ladder of intensity to the climactic point in the chorus. In other words, the recordists created the musical equivalent of the rhetorical figure, *incrementum*.

Example 3.   Words and superstructure, "Laughing"

0:05	*Verse 1*	I should laugh but I cry
		Because your love has passed me by
		You took me by surprise
		You didn't realize that I was waiting
0:29	*Pre-Chorus*	Time goes slowly but carries on
		And now the best years have come and gone
		You took me by surprise
		I didn't realize that you were laughing
0:49	*Chorus 1*	(Laughing) Cause you're doing it to me
		(Laughing) It ain't the way it should be
		You took away everything I had
		You put the hurt on me
0:59		(Laughing) Cause you're doing it to me

		(Laughing) It ain't the way it should be
		You took away everything I had
		You put the hurt on me
1:09	*Verse 2*	I go alone now calling your name
		After losing at the game
		You took me by surprise
		I didn't realize that you were laughing
1:34	*Pre-Chorus*	Time goes slowly but carries on
		And now the best years, the best years have
		come and gone
		You took me by surprise
		I didn't realize that you were laughing
1:54	*Chorus 2*	(Laughing) Cause you're doing it to me
		(Laughing) It ain't the way it should be
		You took away everything I had
		You put the hurt on me
2:05		(Laughing) Cause you're doing it to me
		(Laughing) Ah what you're doin' to me
		You took away everything I had
		You put the hurt on me
2:15	*Outro*	(Laughing) Ha ha ha ha ha ha
		(Laughing) Ha ha ha ha ha ha ha
		(Laughing) Were you laughing at me?
		(Laughing) Were you laughing at me?
		(Laughing) Oh what you're doin' to me, girl
		(Laughing) I'm lookin', you're laughin'
		(Laughing) I'm lookin', you're laughin'
		(Laughing) You're lookin', I'm laughin'
2:39	*track ends*	

Initially, the texture of the first verse remains sparse, for the guitar figure of the intro provides the sole support for the singer. But halfway through the verse, the mix thickens slightly with the addition of a simple bass-guitar line (0:18). The next segment of text functions as a pre-chorus (0:29–0:48) and it is sung to the melody and chord progression of the first verse. The passage the recordists fashion to connect these two sections leads the listener quite smoothly to the second step of the ladder. The rhythmically syncopated repetition of an E-major chord (0:27–0:28; see Example 4), punctuated by the drums, prepares the way for the increased activity of the pre-chorus, and at the moment the chord progression begins to repeat (0:29), background vocals and keyboard are added. This time, however, the rising chromatic line receives greater prominence through its placement in the background vocals, and the guitar, reinforced by a tambourine, accentuates the fourth beat of each bar. The bass outlines the chord tones of the harmonic argument, while the drums present a decorated backbeat pattern.

Example 4.   Connective tissue between verse and pre-chorus, "Laughing"

This enrichment of the texture certainly augments the impact of the song, but because the pre-chorus repeats the harmonic argument and vocal line from the first verse, the rate of change of events remains the same. Clearly, even though the emotional intensity of the song has been advanced, the musical arguments have reached only an intermediate stage. Room exists for further non-textual amplification of the subject, and, not surprisingly, the listener arrives at the top of the ladder in the chorus (0:49–0:59). In placing the greatest concentration of activity at this point, the recordists are able to reinforce the emotional climax of the song, the idea of someone laughing at you after he or she has broken your heart.

The chorus employs one of the commonplaces of popular music, the universal call-and-response topic, and in this application of it, Burton Cummings responds to the other members of the group who sing the word "laughing" (see Example 5). A number of factors contribute to the heightened animation of the section, and one of the ways Bachman and Cummings amplify the subject is through an intensification of the harmonic argument. Up to this point in the song, new harmonies had been introduced slowly, one at the beginning of each bar, but in the chorus, chord changes occur as often as one per beat. The entire section consists of two statements of a four-bar phrase, and in the first and second bars of the phrase (0:49–0:53), bars which are virtually identical, Bachman and Cummings place the progression, D A Bm7, on beats one, two, and three. In the third bar, where they assign chord changes to every other beat, the harmony progresses from D to E before arriving on A in the last bar (0:54–0:59). These frequent changes help propel the chorus forward, and in order to strengthen the section further, the recordists increase the rhythmic activity of the tambourine and introduce a riff-like figure in the guitar to duplicate the vocal line at the words "cause you're doing it to me" and "it ain't the way it should be" (0:50–0:53). As the first statement of the phrase draws to a close, the recordists maintain momentum with a guitar figure designed not only to cover the brief moment of harmonic repose present in the bar but also to connect the two strains firmly together (0:57–0:59).

The energy accumulated in the chorus dissipates in the final bar with the emergence of the introductory guitar figure (1:07). This figure prepares listeners for the second verse but does not return them to the level of intensity they experienced at the beginning of the song. The sustained chords of the keyboard are much more prominent, and the arpeggiated bass line makes the harmony seem less static. Drums, too, are present but the group's drummer, Garry Peterson, at first limits his playing to marking the beats on a closed hi-hat (1:07–1:23). The pre-chorus and

Example 5.   Chorus, first half, "Laughing"

chorus which follow retain their earlier mixes, and the recording ends with a fade on a continuously reiterated line from the chorus (the outro begins at 2:15).

The creative process described here reflects Bachman's general philosophy of teaching songwriting: take a favorite song, keep the chord progression and sing a new melody over it, using the same lyrics; then change the lyrics, phrasing, and breaths; and as a final step, alter the tempo (Einarson and Bachman 2000: 317). Invention and arrangement figure prominently in this approach, and an understanding of the parallels between rhetorical construction and songwriting/recording allows us to place discussions of a record's sonic presence on a continuum of practice that extends back to classical times.[8]

Chapter 6

Transforming a Demo

When Pete Townshend began looking for a project to shape The Who's musical direction in the years immediately following the phenomenal success of *Tommy* (1969), he set aside plans for a conventional album and focused, instead, on a large undertaking that would involve a live musical event, as well as a film, based on what he called a "science-fiction fantasy idea" (Wilkerson 2008: 147). This project, which he later named *Lifehouse*, never reached fruition at the time, for problems plagued it right from the outset. Townshend had difficulty framing his futuristic concept in a way others could understand, and the formidable task of writing a coherent story line that not only would mesh with audience collaboration during a live show but also would work as a film ultimately caused the project to fail.[1] Nonetheless, he had written a number of songs for *Lifehouse*, and when Kit Lambert, The Who's manager/producer, suggested in 1971 that the band join him at the Record Plant in New York to record some of the new songs, Townshend saw this as an opportunity to move the project forward. Indeed, between the 16th and 18th of March, they recorded five of the songs: "Behind Blue Eyes," "Getting in Tune," "Love Ain't for Keeping," "Pure and Easy," and "Won't Get Fooled Again."

During the sessions, however, relations with Kit Lambert deteriorated dramatically, forcing the band to take partially completed tapes back to London, and with no further collaboration with Lambert on the horizon, The Who turned to Glyn Johns for assistance in mixing the Record Plant sessions. But Johns had never thought much of Lambert's engineering abilities, and he persuaded the band to begin anew at Olympic Studios. With Johns at the helm, work on the *Lifehouse* songs commenced on the 9th of April, and by the time they finished recording in June, The Who had enough material for a double concept album. Johns, however, could not be convinced of the viability of a lengthy album centered on the *Lifehouse* story, for he felt the lack of a cohesive narrative in the songs themselves would prevent the plot from being readily understood, especially when presented exclusively in audio format. Townshend, of course, never meant the songs to carry the story line,[2] and this made it impossible for anyone to assemble a logically sequenced concept album. But Johns had a solution to The Who's dilemma: abandon the double disc and issue a single album of disconnected songs from the *Lifehouse* project instead. Track Records released the resulting LP in August, and thanks to Johns' realization of Townshend's pre-production demos *Who's Next* was hailed by John Mendelsohn of *Rolling Stone* as "one of the most masterfully recorded rock records in recent memory" (Wilkerson 2008: 170–71).

In fact, Townshend commented in 1983 that "*Who's Next* [was] one of the best sounding Who albums because . . . the demos I made to accompany the *Lifehouse* film script I wrote in '71 are among the best I have ever produced" (Wilkerson 2008: 150, 171). His demos had always provided a detailed plan for The Who to follow when recording new songs, and in 1999 Glyn Johns praised the excellence of Townshend's pre-production

work: "Pete's demos were always fantastic and were always a challenge
. . . very often I'd listen to the song that we were about to cut and I'd go,
'How the hell am I going to compete with that?' Really, really brilliant
demos" (ibid.: 150). Johns certainly rose to this challenge, for even though
Townshend thought he had "good songs and good ideas" for *Lifehouse*,
he recognized the degree to which "our producer [Johns] stuck his neck
out to enhance and evolve not just the songs, but also the *sounds* I had
produced at home" (ibid.: 171). Townshend subsequently released two of
these demos on *Scoop* in 1983 ("Bargain" and "Behind Blue Eyes"), and
his meticulous pre-production work on "Behind Blue Eyes" demonstrates
how the basic plan he established in his home studio came to fruition in
the presence of different producers. Both Lambert and Johns followed the
musical direction Townshend set out in the demo, yet The Who deemed
only the track produced in London as worthy of release, despite a great
deal of similarity between the versions of "Behind Blue Eyes" recorded
at the Record Plant and Olympic Studios. Johns, of course, originally
was brought in just to remix and add overdubs to the New York material, but since he felt he could do a better job if the band started again,
the enhancements he brought to Townshend's demo, when viewed from
the perspective of Lambert's rejected contributions, reveals the degree
to which subtle changes of musical detail can affect the aesthetic appeal
of a recording.

In the liner notes to *Scoop*, Townshend discussed the heightened
intensity the band brought to the demo and addressed the relationship
of "Behind Blue Eyes" to the *Lifehouse* story:

> Another LIFEHOUSE song — I remember my wife saying she liked this
> one from the kitchen below after I had finished the harmony vocals.
> The band later added a passion and a fire that really made it blossom
> from the sad song it appears to be here [on *Scoop*] into the proud self
> exposé it became on WHO'S NEXT. Not a personal song at all, or at least

not intended to be. It's about the villain in the story feeling he is forced into playing a two-faced role. (Townshend 2000)

Apparently, Townshend never intended "Behind Blue Eyes" to be autobiographical, but by 1982 a personal connection had become clear to him:

> [The song] was written about a man who actually was a villain and he seemed to be a villain; he's accused of being a liar and a cheat, when in fact his motives are absolutely pure . . . So I tried to capture this character that I'd written and then realised it was me afterwards, and about a part of me that I hadn't considered: the inability to be taken literally because of the way people take you to be. You can never define, you can never control how people react to you, however much of a star you think you are. You can never hide what you really are. (Wilkerson 2008: 166–67)

The intensely sad lyrics, then, found new meaning in the hands of the band and their producers, recordists who augmented the persuasiveness of the song by reinforcing, amplifying, and refining the basic elements of Townshend's demo.

Townshend conceived "Behind Blue Eyes" more as a ballad than one of the hard-driving rock numbers normally associated with The Who, and its superstructure consists of a short intro followed by a verse/chorus complex of 34 bars, a bridge of equal size, and a four-bar outro (see Examples 1 and 2 for charts which show the disposition of the song's sections, as well as prominent features of the three versions considered here). On the demo, a nylon-strung acoustic guitar provides chordal accompaniment for each section, the verses and choruses receiving an arpeggiated treatment and the bridge featuring a vigorous dotted rhythm applied to block harmonies. Townshend derives his chords from the E-Aeolian mode and incorporates both major and minor triads above the first and fifth steps of the scale so that the verses center on Em, the cho-ruses on E, and the bridge on the triadically neutral E5 (see Example 2). These contrasting focal points help differentiate the various sections of the song, and the way in which he approaches the modal center of each unit further defines its harmonic palette. He chooses to build chords on the 1st, 3rd, 4th, 5th, 6th, and 7th steps of the scale, and in the verses he employs a five-chord progression, 1 3 7 6 4, which drives to the minor triad at the core of every verse through 7 6 4 motion. The two choruses, on the other hand, use three and four chord sequences that reverse the 7 6 harmonic progression to approach the modal center, E, through 6 7 or 6 7 4 motions. The bridge also utilizes three-chord groupings as struc-tural blocks, but unlike the verses and choruses, the bridge prominently features chords built on the fifth step of the scale in 1 5 4, 7 5 4, or 5 4 7 progressions, the last of these sequences employing a major triad instead of a minor one on the fifth step. The 5 4 movement at the heart of each tri-chord structure not only establishes the harmonic character of the section but also provides additional contrast to the verse/chorus complex, that is, differentiation beyond the rhythmic figure which underpins the chord progressions in the bridge.

Example 1. Structure, lyrics, and prominent recorded features of "Behind Blue Eyes"

	Lyrics	Demo	Record Plant Sessions	Who's Next
Intro		ac gtr (nylon strings) 2 statements of short arp figure (2 bars)	ac gtr (steel strings) short arp figure (1 bar)	ac gtr (steel strings) long arp figure (2 bars)
V1	No one knows what it's like / To be the bad man / To be the sad man	0:07 vcl sgl tr; ac gtr arp	0:03 vcl sgl tr; ac gtr arp	0:07 vcl sgl tr; ac gtr arp
	Behind blue eyes	line reinforced by bup vcls	line reinforced by bup vcls	line reinforced by bup vcls
V2	No one knows what it's like / To be hated / To be fated	0:22 vcl sgl tr; ac gtr arp	0:18 vcl sgl tr; ac gtr arp	0:22 vcl sgl tr; ac gtr arp
	To telling only lies	line reinforced by bup vcls	line reinforced by bup vcls	line reinforced by bup vcls
Ch	But my dreams / They aren't as empty / As my conscience seems / to be	0:36 vcl dbl tr; ac gtr arp	0:32 cymbal roll; vcl dbl tr; simple bass; sus organ chords; ac gtr arp. ac gtr sgl strummed fill	0:37 vcl dbl tr; active bass (prominent); ac gtr strums chords. ac gtr strummed fills

	Demo		Record Plant Sessions		Who's Next	
I have hours, only lonely My love is vengeance That's never free				ac gtr strummed fills		ac gtr strummed fills
V3	No one knows what it's like To feel these feelings Like I do	1:09	vcl sgl tr; ac gtr arp	1:06	bup vcls reinforce lead vcl; simple bass; sus organ chords; ac gtr arp	1:13	vcl dbl tr, lightly harm; "ooo" in bup vcls; active bass (prominent); ac gtr arp
	And I blame you		line reinforced by bup vcls		line reinforced by bup vcls, but less rich than verses 1 & 2		line reinforced by bup vcls, but less rich than verses 1 & 2
V4	No one bites back as hard On their anger None of my pain and woe	1:24	vcl sgl tr; ac gtr arp	1:20	vcl lightly harm; simple bass; sus organ chords; ac gtr arp.	1:28	vcl dbl tr, lightly harm; "ooo" in bup vcls; active bass (prominent); ac gtr arp

(continued)

Example 1. (*cont.*)

		Demo	Record Plant Sessions	Who's Next
	Can show through	line reinforced by bup vcls	line reinforced by bup vcls, but less rich than verses 1 & 2	line reinforced by bup vcls, but less rich than verses 1 & 2
Ch	But my dreams They aren't as empty As my conscience seems to be	1:38 vcl dbl tr; ac gtr arp	1:34 cymbal roll; vcl dbl tr & lightly harm; simple bass; sus organ chords; ac gtr arp ac gtr strummed & el gtr sgl fill	1:43 vcl harm; active bass (prominent); ac gtr strums chords ac gtr strummed fills
	I have hours, only lonely My love is vengeance			vcl dbl tr (no harm)
	That's never free		"free" harm ac gtr strummed & el gtr fills	"free" harm ac gtr strummed fills

		Demo		Record Plant Sessions		Who's Next	
Br	When my fist clenches, crack it open	2:19	vcl dbl tr; prominent dotted rhythm in ac gtr	2:16	el gtr solo frames bridge; vcl sgl tr; full drums; el gtr licks throughout; organ chords; ac gtr & bass play demo rhythm (subdued)	2:27	el gtr solo frames bridge; vcl dbl tr; full drums; ac gtr, el gtr, & bass play demo rhythm (prominent); el gtr fill between halves
	Before I use it and lose my cool						
	When I smile, tell me some bad news						
	Before I laugh and act like a fool						
	And if I swallow anything evil	2:36	vcl harm	2:33	bup vcls reinforce lead vcl (mixed low)	2:45	bup vcls reinforce lead vcl (mixed low)
	Put your finger down my throat						
	And if I shiver, please give me a blanket		[Townshend sings: "But if . . ."]				
	Keep me warm, let me wear your coat						
		2:56	instrumental extension of bridge	2:53	instrumental extension of bridge	3:06	instrumental extension of bridge

(continued)

Example 1. (*cont.*)

		Demo	Record Plant Sessions	Who's Next
Outro (V1)	No one knows what it's like To be the bad man To be the sad man Behind blue eyes	3:10 vcl dbl tr; ac gtr arp line reinforced by bup vcls 3:25 track ends	3:07 vcl sgl tr; sus organ chords; ac gtr arp; active bass line reinforced by bup vcls & cymbal splash on each word 3:25 track ends	3:20 vcl dbl tr; ac gtr arp; active bass (prominent) line reinforced by bup vcls & cymbal splash on each word 3:39 track ends

ac = acoustic

arp = arpeggiated/arpeggiation

bup = backup

dbl = double

el = electric

gtr = guitar

harm = harmonized/harmonization

sgl = single

sus = sustained

tr = tracked

vcl = vocal

Example 2. Scale and chord progressions (normalized, as many of the chords in the bridge anticipate the beginning of the bar)

Scale:

					b		
b		d	e	f♯	g	a	b
g/g♯			c♯	d/d♯	e	f♯	g/g♯
E	F♯	G	A	B	C	D	E	⇒ E-Aeolian

Intro (2 bars)

E^{5sus4} | E^{5sus4} |

Verse/Chorus Complex (34 bars)

Verses 1 & 2 (8 bars)

||: E^m G^5 | D | C^{maj7} | A^{5sus2} :||

Chorus (8 bars + 1 bar extension)

C D | G^5 | C D^{5sus2} | E | B^m | C | D D^{5sus2} | A^{5sus2} | A^{5sus2} |

Verses 3 & 4 (8 Bars)

||: E^m G^5 | D | C^{add9} | A^{5sus2} :||

Chorus (8 bars + 1 bar extension)

C D | G^5 | C D | E | B^m | C | D D^{5sus2} | A^{5sus2} | A^{5sus2} |

Bridge (34 bars)

E^5 | B^m A ||: E^5 | B^m A | E^5 | B^m A | E^5 | B^m G^5 | D^5 |
B^m A | D^5 | B^m A :||
E^5 | B^m A | E^5 | B^m A | B A | D^5 D^{5sus2} | B A | D^5 D^{5sus2} |
B A | D^5 D^{5sus2} | B | A |

Outro: Verse 1 (4 bars)

$E^m G^5$ | D | C^{maj7} | A^5 ||

Townshend further distinguishes the song's divisions through a judicious application of single and double tracking in which he single tracks the vocal in the verses and gives the choruses a thicker, more intense sound by doubling the voice. He employs this technique in the bridge, as well, but broadens the texture during the second half of the section through harmonization, a procedure he also applies to the last line of each verse. For the verse passages, however, he chose to reinforce the concluding sentiments not with a single extra voice but with richer harmonies comprised of more than one part. This basic plan provided the blueprint for the recordists to flesh out in the studio, yet The Who found somewhat different ways to realize the potential of the song in New York and London.

In both studio versions, Townshend altered the arpeggiation he had played on the demo and substituted a steel-strung acoustic guitar for the nylon-strung one he had used at home. The arpeggio pattern became less four-square, gaining a fluidity that the demo lacked (aided by a more natural sounding accentuation, particularly on *Who's Next*), and whereas Townshend reduced the length of the intro to a single bar at the Record Plant, he restored the opening to its original duration in London (see Example 3). On the two recordings, the arpeggiated figures continue in the first and second verses, and just like the demo, the recordists single track the vocal and reinforce the final line of both verses through harmonization. At the outset of the first chorus, however, the New York and London versions begin to diverge. Although each one contains a doubled lead vocal, a cymbal roll accompanies the opening words of the Record Plant chorus, and the sustained organ chords played by Al Kooper, who sat in on the New York sessions, act as pads behind Townshend's guitar arpeggiation and the simple bass line supplied by John Entwistle. The

London sessions, on the other hand, proceeded without an organ, and Townshend decided to replace the organ pads, as well as the arpeggiation he had used earlier, with rhythmic strumming, while Entwistle provided a much more active bass part, a line which the recordists subsequently mixed prominently. But beyond these enhancements, Townshend created additional excitement and passion in London by modifying the strummed guitar fills he had devised in New York for the midpoint and end of the chorus, primarily through crisper rhythms and more conspicuous syncopation, features his Record Plant performances lacked.

Example 3.   Intro figuration for "Behind Blue Eyes"

The ensuing third and fourth verses do not return to the emotional plane of the initial stanzas, for in both New York and London the recordists chose to build upon the texture established in the chorus, albeit to a greater degree at Olympic Studios. On the Record Plant recording, even though several aspects of the arrangement retain the flavor of the chorus, particularly the acoustic guitar arpeggiation, sustained organ chords, and simple bass part, the lead vocal is reinforced by a backup singer who doubles Roger Daltrey's line in the third verse and lightly harmonizes it in the fourth. The London sessions fortify the vocals even further, because the recordists not only apply double tracking and light harmonization to Daltrey's part in both verses but also place a stack of voices singing "ooo" behind it. Townshend, on the other hand, returns to an arpeggiated accompaniment to help differentiate these verses from the chorus, and in a manner similar to the Record Plant sessions, the final lines of the stanzas receive less reinforcement than before.

On both recordings, however, the return of the chorus encouraged the recordists to heighten its emotional intensity in preparation for the bridge, the climax of the song. Although the basic arrangements from the previous chorus did not change, they found new ways to heighten the effect of Daltrey's voice. At the Record Plant, double tracking and light harmonization differentiated this section from the preceding ones, and in London, a harmonized lead vocal gave way to a double-tracked line without backing harmonies. Curiously, an electric guitar fill suddenly appears at the midpoint of the section on the New York recording, but during the London sessions, the recordists reserved Townshend's electric guitar for the bridge, probably to provide a stark contrast to the harmonized melodic extension of the word "free" that not only closes the second chorus but also leads the listener to anticipate a new musical event. Townshend does not disappoint, for the pace of the recording shifts abruptly at this point.

Indeed, the introduction of an aggressive, heavily distorted guitar part, together with a full drum kit and a sharply defined chordal underlay, launched the climactic section dramatically at Olympic Studios. But, unfortunately, the bridge never reached its full potential in New York. The recordists had interjected the electric guitar prematurely, robbing themselves of the opportunity to set the bridge apart timbrally, and the subdued delivery of the underlying harmonies weakened the effect of the strong chord progression Townshend had composed. On top of this, the single-tracked vocal lacked the force the words required, and the electric guitar licks Townshend played throughout the bridge contributed little to the cohesion of the section. But the band certainly remedied these deficiencies in London, for not only did the addition of an electric guitar to the underlying chord progression help fortify and sharpen the rhythmic character of the accompaniment beyond what a bass and acoustic guitar could achieve on their own but also the strident quality of Daltrey's voice, which was double tracked, imbued the words with the sort of vehemence they seemed to demand. Moreover, other than the short fill Townshend inserted at the midpoint of the bridge to mask a moment of repose, he restricted his solo guitar work to the two instrumental passages which bookend the section, the second of which he extends by 14 seconds in a repeated harmonic drive to the seventh step of the scale that dissipates its energy across a 5 4 1 progression in preparation for a return to the opening verse.

At the end of this transition, the texture thins considerably on both recordings, and the restatement of the first verse, which functions as an outro, rounds out the superstructure of the song through the rhetorical figure, *epanalepsis* (a device in which a unit begins and ends with the same word or words). Townshend places an expression of importance at the beginning of the song to be considered and at the end to be remembered in order to leave listeners with a weighty matter to ponder. This final section more or less recaptures the emotional plane of the third and fourth verses, except that in New York the vocal was single tracked, while Entwistle played a more active bass part, and in London the recordists dropped the stack of supporting "ooo's." Cymbal splashes accompany each harmonized word in the final line, and this accentuates and draws attention to the central proposition considered in the song, the character of the individual behind blue eyes.

In crafting their tracks, the recordists began with Townshend's meticulous, yet unpretentious, demo and enhanced its emotional appeal by adding, in Townshend's own words, "a passion and a fire that really made it blossom from the sad song it appears to be here [on *Scoop*] into the

Chapter 7

Hit-and-Miss Affair

The art of crafting successful pop singles can be a hit-and-miss affair, as The Who's first efforts to record "Behind Blue Eyes" aptly demonstrate, and for many people in the recording industry the most important component of a commercially viable record is a great song.[1] But because songs destined for the Top 40 market need to be turned into appealing records, musicians often remark on the importance of clothing songs in striking arrangements. "The arrangement is everything that makes a hit record," suggests Richard Carpenter, "you can have the best singer on the planet and the best song, but if you don't have the right arrangement for that song and singer, the singer's going nowhere and so is the song" (Olsen *et al.* 1999: 115). Burt Bacharach phrases the notion somewhat differently. "You can have a hell of a song," he says, "and have it spoiled by a bad arrangement or production . . . you need the right showcase" (Saal 1970: 51). These comments probably could be applied to any number of well-written songs that failed to chart, but one in particular, Bacharach and David's "(They Long to Be) Close to You," aptly illustrates the points they make. Bacharach's first two attempts at producing the song, one with Richard Chamberlain in 1963 and the other with Dionne Warwick the following year, were, and still are, considered artistic failures.[2] In fact, the full potential of the song remained unrealized until 1970 when, without input from Bacharach, Richard and Karen Carpenter turned "Close to You" into a hit that reached number one in the USA and spent four weeks at the top of the *Billboard* charts.

These three versions of "Close to You" demonstrate the vital role arrangements play in determining the artistic merit of a recording, and by comparing Bacharach's failed versions with the Carpenters' successful rendition of the song, I anchor the notion of hits and misses to Carpenter's and Bacharach's insistence that a great song cannot become a hit without the "right" arrangement. In short, I investigate how recordists either enhance (Carpenters) or diminish (Bacharach) the impact of the story told in the lyrics through the creation and release of emotional and musical tension, the expressive flow of a recording. I take my cue here from Burt Bacharach himself, for in an interview with Paul Zollo dating from 1997, he discusses the failure of "Close to You" in relation to its musical properties: "I'm very grateful to Richard Carpenter making that record the way that they heard it. Because the way that I heard it was very different and not very good. I made the first few records of it with the wrong groove, wrong feel. Richard came in and nailed it" (2003: 209).[3] He has always openly acknowledged his "misses," and in an interview with Bill DeMain he said that "the first record [of 'Close to You'] with Richard Chamberlain . . . was a terrible record. I had a terrible arrangement and a terrible concept" (1997).[4]

As discussed earlier, musicians generally shape arrangements either privately in individual workspaces or collaboratively during the recording process, and in cases where demos and other preliminary versions have been released, such as with "Behind Blue Eyes," researchers can readily study the creative process that led to the final mix, that is, the ultimate interpretation of a song, issued on disc. But when no demos, outtakes, or other preliminary arrangements are available for scrutiny, compositional practices can be uncovered only from the released version, and in the absence of testimony from the recordists involved, studies of this sort must remain speculative. However, when a producer like Burt Bacharach recorded one of his own songs with more than one artist and worked from the same basic arrangement each time, the recordings themselves reveal the ways in which the musical material has been altered in an effort to capture that elusive hit.

Without a doubt, Bacharach's two early versions of "Close to You" failed to excite the interest of listeners, even though the second recording had a much better singer in Dionne Warwick and Bacharach had improved the arrangement. But as the Carpenters aptly demonstrated in 1970, the song itself was not the problem, for Bacharach had composed memorable tunes and rich harmonies to which Hal David had added, to borrow Serene Dominic's words, "clever lines about birds and stars going out of their way to be close to you" (2003: 110) (see Example 1).[5] David's lyric style, however, consisted of much more than clever lines, for he sought to incorporate in his writing some of the features he admired in the lyrics of Cole Porter, Irving Berlin, Oscar Hammerstein, Lorenz Hart, and Johnny Mercer, that is, believability, simplicity, and emotional impact (David).[6] "Close to You" embraces all three of these qualities and presents an uncomplicated story readily familiar to most people, the infatuation of a boy for a girl. But instead of developing his story in a linear fashion, David utilizes Bacharach's verse/bridge structure to reveal a fully realized scenario in careful, logical stages. The parallel structure of the two introductory verses, replete with teasers in the form of questions, illustrate rather than state directly the central emotion of the lyric, and the unpretentious imagery of these verses (birds suddenly appearing and stars falling down from the sky) not only explains why the central figure of the song is so popular but also prepares listeners for the climactic moment in the bridge. Here the speaker gushes effusively about angels creating his dream come true, and the energy that accumulates across the five lines of this emotional climax dissipates in the third verse when the speaker concludes "that is why all the boys in town follow you all around."

Example 1.   Lyrics, "(They Long to Be) Close to You"

Verse 1	Why do birds suddenly appear
	Ev'ry time you are near?
	Just like me
	They long to be
	Close to you
Verse 2	Why do stars fall down from the sky
	Ev'ry time you walk by?
	Just like me
	They long to be
	Close to you
Bridge	On the day that you were born
	The angels got together and decided
	To create a dream come true
	So they sprinkled moon dust in your hair
	Of gold and starlight in your eyes of blue
Verse 3	That is why all the boys in town
	Follow you all around
	Just like me
	They long to be
	Close to you
Outro	Just like me
	They long to be
	Close to you

In crafting their song, then, Bacharach and David seem to have restricted the emotional ebb and flow of the drama to two levels of intensity, one for the verses and another for the bridge. The uniformity of sentiment expressed in the verses, facilitated by both a refrain ("just like me, they long to be close to you") and an unvarying musical setting, contrasts sharply with the rising tension of the bridge, tension engendered by a melodic line which ascends in three stages until it reaches a culminating peak on the final word (see Example 2). But in order for the recordists to transform the structural foundation of the song into effective musical discourse, they needed to enhance the basic framework provided by the songwriters, and in liberating the composition from its relatively inexpressive form, the musicians involved added the rhythmic flexibility that composers rarely try to capture in their notation (see Example 3, as well as note 11) and clothed the raw song in arrangements intended to create a satisfying dramatic flow. Both Bacharach and Carpenter found their own ways of distributing musical ideas and instruments within the mix, but Bacharach's first attempts at realizing "Close to You" on disc, by his own admission, missed the mark.

Example 2.   Bridge of "(They Long to Be) Close to You" (as published)

In fairness to Bacharach, however, his sessions with Chamberlain and Warwick were constrained by the recording practices of the day. In the early 1960s, producers usually had to work quickly in the studio and in

Bacharach's own words he often had to execute "a whole arrangement, right on the spot. Good or bad or whatever, it was there" ("Bacharach & David" 1978: 8). Phil Ramone remembers the pressure producers like Bacharach were under at his own A&R Studios in New York: "In those days, we used to do three-hour sessions, and . . . in three hours you were supposed to cut at least four songs . . . As an engineer, I was constantly looking at the clock and you had to be able to get a balance in an amazingly short time. If you couldn't balance a rhythm section and pull up a good level on the horns within five minutes, you were not considered good enough to work with the pros. So the clock often determined what a record would sound like" (Cunningham 1998: 59). Obviously, Bacharach had to work expeditiously to get good performances out of his musicians, and even though he repeatedly used the same nucleus of musicians and had learned to remedy deficiencies in an arrangement quite quickly in the studio (Rudman 1964b: 18), Steve Tyrell, a staff producer at Scepter Records, remembers that "those records were recorded live, all at one time — with Dionne singing, the strings playing, the horns playing, the rhythm section, and the background vocals. Everybody was in there, and Burt was standing in the middle" (Platts 2003: 46).[7] Bacharach confirmed in an interview in 1970 that he preferred recording "live, like a crap game, with everyone hearing everyone else at the same time" instead of making records piecemeal (Saal 1970: 52).

Bacharach had gradually managed to gain complete control over his sessions, one of the main reasons he decided to produce his own songs in the first place,[8] and in 1964 Hal David spoke of the meticulous way in which he and Burt worked: "before we even think of recording we completely finish and polish the strongest song we feel we can write at that time . . . it often takes from two to three months to produce a single record. This includes the inception of a song, through thorough rehearsing, careful planning of [the] arrangement and careful planning of the choral background" (Rudman 1964a: 14). Later in the same interview,

Bacharach elaborated on David's comments: "we take three days to two weeks to compose a song, working separately and together. We hear the song over 400 times . . . [and] when we feel it is right and have taught the song to the artist and thoroughly rehearsed the performance, we're up to about 450 listenings. I then go home and plan the arrangement which gives me another 80 listenings." All this preparation certainly paid off, for Gene Pitney recalled the thrill of working with Bacharach in the studio: "his command [of the orchestra at Bell Sound Studios in New York] was electrifying. The musicians had so much respect that they would be absolutely quiet and do his every bidding . . . to watch the masters [Bacharach and David] at work while I was singing the vocals was a complete rush that prompted that extra 10 per cent out of my performance" (Platts 2003: 20–21). Bacharach often recorded dozens of takes, admitting to as many as twenty-four in his 1964 interview with *Billboard*, and many years later when speaking of the recording session for "Alfie" with Cilla Black he said, "I was very hard on the singer. I don't think she knew what hit her. We must have gone 28 or 29 takes with her [looking for] that little bit more" (Brocken 2003: 182). In fact, Bacharach allowed most singers very little musical freedom during recording sessions, for even though rehearsals leading to a recording date might induce Bacharach to make small changes to a song, Dionne Warwick recalled that "by and large, whatever [Bacharach and David] wrote was what they wrote and that's what we sang" (Platts 2003: 32). Rose Marie Jun, one of Bacharach's backing singers in the late 1960s, concurs:

[He was in] total control, all the time. He knew absolutely what he wanted. He knew the phrasing he wanted, he knew the way he wanted the words to go. He knew exactly the way he wanted it performed, and we did it pretty much the way he wanted it . . . The phrasing — he'd have certain little ways of saying the words himself, and he wanted you to do it that way . . . Richard Rodgers was the same way — he wanted

it exactly the way it was written — no changes, not a dot different . . .
With Burt, you could say, "Well, couldn't I do it this way?" He'd give
it some thought but generally you did it the way he wanted it done.
(Platts 2003: 63)

Similarly, B. J. Thomas remembers his rehearsal with Bacharach just prior
to recording "Raindrops Keep Fallin' on My Head":

I have some vocal tricks that I do, running around the notes . . . and he
just told me straight out. He said "B. J., after you do this song and all
the notes exactly like I've written them, if you have any space to do that,
well, feel free." So really the only place where I could kind of play with
the melody was at the end, where I did the [sings] "me-e-e-e-ee . . ."
And when I did that in the studio, he was conducting the orchestra and
he kind of looked over his shoulder at me . . . and he said, "Oh, okay,
that works." So, he didn't allow me to use much of my style. Basically I
just sang his notes. (Platts 2003: 72)

As these singers demonstrate, Bacharach notated his songs meticulously, Carole Bayer Sager stating that his penchant for precision could
sometimes irritate the lyricist working with him:

In the beginning of "That's What Friends Are For" . . . [Burt] goes "no,
that's da-dum." [I said] "What's the difference, just get rid of the 'da-
dum' and go into . . ." I got so pissed-off, it's just a 16th note — what does
it matter? . . . He was so precise about it, it was so important to him and
he sits in the music room and spends an hour on whether he wanted the
16th note. If you are the lyricist [it] could be rather maddening. But, he
was right, and I finally wrote "and I." (Brocken 2003: 233)

Bacharach's attention to detail became legendary among the artists he produced,[9] so much so that it is probably safe to assume that his initial recordings of "Close to You" remained firmly in his control.

The arrangement he wrote for the song, despite his public insistence in 1964 that he and David planned all aspects of a recording meticulously, centers on a groove he later admitted did not evoke the right feel, and critics have certainly noticed this, especially on the Chamberlain recording, where prominent piano chords in the accompaniment pulse on eighth notes at a tempo of 72 bpm.[10] The pianist's *staccato* manner of playing these chords generates a rigid quality which Bacharach foregrounds, and simple drum and acoustic bass parts contribute to the tedium of the groove (the snare provides a straight backbeat while the bass emphasizes beats one and three). Unfortunately, Chamberlain's mechanistic singing seems to reinforce the rhythmic monotony of the accompaniment, and because Bacharach did not use an instrumental introduction to define the groove, the first few notes Chamberlain sings are crucially important. But instead of beginning the song with a clear rhythmic impetus, Bacharach placed pause signs above the first two notes, and Chamberlain, following the notation precisely, lengthened these notes as he sang them. Strings provide the backdrop for this introductory gesture, and Bacharach's decision to double the singer with single notes played on an electric guitar does little to entice the listener into the sonic world of the song. The sparse instrumentation that follows (piano, acoustic bass, and drums), coupled to the languid opening and monotonous groove, prevents the song from making a satisfactory impression in the critical first fifteen to twenty seconds.

Bacharach retains this basic arrangement in the second verse but thickens the texture with the addition of a counter melody in the strings, and in order to hide a moment of stasis in the half bar that separates the verses, he inserts arpeggiated chords on successive beats, first on the piano and then on the guitar. A much larger gap of a full bar exists between the second verse and the bridge, and even though many recordists would consider this an obvious place to build tension in preparation for the emotional climax of the song, Bacharach's arrangement does not drive forward at this point. A short horn fill, followed in the strings by a heavily emphasized harmonic descent from dominant to tonic, barely provides adequate musical resources for leading the listener imperceptibly from one level to the next. The bridge itself begins innocuously with a simple stepwise counter melody in the strings that pushes upwards in the second phrase to the climactic passage in the last two bars. Here, the pulsing eighth notes in all parts, augmented by Chamberlain's most impassioned singing, represent the climax of the recording. The energy accumulated across the bridge then dissipates in two piano *glissandi* that return listeners to the emotional plane of the earlier verses, and not surprisingly Bacharach disposes his instrumental backdrop in a manner very similar to those verses, even though he varies the string writing somewhat. A single repetition of the refrain, joined to the third verse through a horn fill, functions as the outro and gradually fades to draw the song to a close.

Although Bacharach eventually acknowledged that this arrangement was a miscalculation, initially he must have been satisfied with much of his work on the song, because he retained many features of the Chamberlain version when he produced Dionne Warwick's recording the following year. Warwick had become a favorite singer of Bacharach and David, and her natural vocal delivery suited their songs well. In fact, despite her protestations to the contrary quoted above, Bacharach granted her the rare privilege of interpreting his melodies as she saw fit, and in 1966 he acknowledged that he no longer made suggestions to her, for he had come to realize that whatever she sang would be a "jewel" (Saal 1966: 102; Wilson 1968: D17). As Warwick recalled decades later, "they were the songwriters and I was the interpreter" (O'Brien 2002: 91), and since her interpretive sensibilities were derived from the normal accentuation of spoken words, especially with regard to the rhythmic structure she had always imposed on Bacharach's melodies, her prosodic singing style contrasted sharply with that of Richard Chamberlain. Chamberlain preferred the type of vocal delivery practiced by numerous crooners and opera singers, and he regularly elongated vowels, holding many notes for their full value, and rarely shaped individual notes dynamically, either by swelling into or tapering off them. Moreover, he cemented successive notes together to produce what could best be described as a true *legato* style with no break in sound and used *vibrato* on every note long enough to admit it. Warwick, on the other hand, sang with much more dynamic shading and controlled her *vibrato* carefully, frequently beginning longer notes with a straight tone before adding a slow vibration. And because her delivery was much more closely aligned to speaking, she rarely adhered to the mechanical way the vocal lines had been notated, even though she did hold the last notes of phrases close to the length Bacharach had indicated. However, Chamberlain also used speech-like rhythms on occasion, especially when Bacharach's melody contained shorter values (see Example 3), but in the second half of the bridge, both singers adhered to the robotic pulsing of the chordal accompaniment.

Nonetheless, despite the differences in vocal style between the two singers, Bacharach decided to preserve the tempo and basic flavor of the original groove in the second recording, particularly the pulsing eighth-note chords played on the piano (a chart which compares the recordings appears in Example 4). But because these chords were placed in a higher register and were performed with a light *legato* touch, the accompaniment sounded less robotic, and the removal of the snare from the backbeat further helped establish, to borrow Bacharach's words, a better feel. Apart from this improvement, however, the languorous introduction remained more or less the same, except that a cymbal splash preceded the first two notes of the vocal and a vibraphone replaced the electric guitar. The addition of the vibraphone certainly resulted in a softer, more blended sound, but the rest of the first verse retained the instrumentation of the

Example 3.   Speech-like (prosodic) rhythms in "(They Long to Be) Close
to You" (the first line appears as published, and the other two
lines are transcribed from the recordings by Chamberlain and
Warwick)

earlier recording. Bacharach seems to have been satisfied with other
features of Chamberlain's version, as well, because in the second verse
of the Warwick recording, even though he gave the strings a subdued
quality, he kept the figuration of his original arrangement. The transi-
tions between sections, however, clearly dissatisfied him, for instead of
hiding the moment of stasis between the first two verses with arpeggiated
chords, he used a flowing horn melody, and in the full bar that separates
the second verse from the bridge, he substituted a tympani roll for the
exaggerated string gesture. This new figure provided an effective ramp
to the heightened tension of the bridge, but unlike the Chamberlain

recording, where Bacharach intensified this contrasting section as it progressed, Warwick's version maintains a uniform texture and level of intensity throughout (achieved in part by the backup singers doubling the counter melody in the strings and the tympanist decorating the first and third beats of each bar). Bacharach then dissipated the accumulated energy of the bridge in the same way that he did on the Chamberlain recording: two piano *glissandi* transport listeners to the third verse and return them to the instrumental backdrop and emotional plane of the opening. The recording closes with an outro similarly restricted to a single repetition of the refrain, but in Warwick's case, backup singers carry the main melody while she echoes and decorates the tune in a quasi call-and-response manner. This creates a much more satisfactory close to the song, and the Warwick recording, despite Bacharach's decision to retain many features of the original arrangement, was decidedly better than the Chamberlain version. Nevertheless, Bacharach and David felt that they still hadn't found the "right rendition," and artistic and commercial success continued to elude the song until Herb Alpert, to whom David had sent a copy of Warwick's version of "Close to You" (in response to a request for a song that hadn't been a hit but which still haunted him), suggested to Richard Carpenter, one of his label's new artists, that he work up an arrangement (Coleman 1994: 82–83; Platts 2003: 76–77).

On his website, Carpenter describes in considerable detail several features of his arrangement, as well as his initial reaction to the song:

I'd been given the lead sheet of this little-known Bacharach-David song by Herb Alpert, who wanted me to work up an arrangement. We were set up on the A&M sound stage at the time. I took the lead sheet, put it on my Wurlitzer, came up with a slow shuffle, the modulation, trumpet solo etc. All the while, I have to tell you, I'm not exactly taken with this song (I've been saying this for 36 years; it took a while to grow on me.) I was doing this because I had been asked by Herb. I got to the end of

it, and working with the lead sheet, which is just something basic for
an arranger to work with, it ended, "Just like me, they long to be close
to you." I'm thinking "this needs something more." I didn't want to end
just like the intro; it just wasn't strong enough. I always liked records
with arrangements that had something at the end that came out of left
field; just when you thought the record was over, something out of left
field shows up. A perfect example is by Bacharach himself on the end
of "Raindrops Keep Falling On My Head." That's where I got the idea
of the ending for "Close To You;" I composed the "wah" bit.

Ultimately, the arrangement concluded with two endings; to "bookend" it I played the same riff as the intro, albeit in A flat and not in C.
The first time one heard the recording, he or she for a split second,
would think it was done. But wait, there was more. For as strong as the
song and arrangement are, for as well as every person involved sang
and played until that point, try thinking of it ending without that tag.
I'm not certain "Close To You" would have been quite the hit it was.
(Carpenter)

In discussing some of the ways he breathed life into the song, to borrow Bacharach's analogy (Platts 2003: 77), Carpenter focuses his attention
on the arrangement, especially the tag he composed to provide a stronger
ending to the recording, and his comments allow us to understand his
craft from an arranger's perspective. He first mentions the groove, a slow
shuffle, and then he lists several other facets of the arrangement (modulation, trumpet solo, tag, and intro riff) that differentiate his interpretation
from Bacharach's. The slow shuffle on which he bases the song, however,
actually operates at a faster tempo than Bacharach had chosen (87 bpm
instead of 72), yet Carpenter's version, clocking in at 3:37, was over
a minute longer than either the Chamberlain recording (2:16) or the
Warwick version (2:21). Undoubtedly, Carpenter felt he needed a longer
more nuanced structure to create an expressive flow that would enhance

the story told in the lyrics in a way that a shorter treatment of the song could not. Hence, he added an instrumental introduction, modulated from C to D flat at the trumpet solo, repeated the bridge and third verse, and composed two endings to be heard in succession. The first ending simply restated the piano introduction in A flat, while the second introduced new material which in Carpenter's own words "came out of left field." The chart in Example 4 schematically represents the differences between the two approaches.

Carpenter's introduction defines the groove right at the outset, and the attractive piano riff he devised, with its gently swinging triplet feel, engages the listener immediately. He adds a vibraphone halfway through, and this exemplifies one of the general principles Carpenter follows in his arrangements — add or subtract sonic events at significant structural moments in order to create or release musical and emotional tension. As his short nine-second intro draws to a close, the vocal emerges from the final chord. Gone are the pauses Bacharach had stipulated for the first two notes of the verse, and Carpenter's piano accompaniment, which pulses on quarter-note chords played midrange on the instrument, not only continues the relaxed feel of the intro but also provides the sole accompaniment for the singer's delivery of the first verse. Karen sings this verse in a prosodic vocal style, and just like Dionne Warwick, she separates notes from one another and keeps the last notes of phrases short (except for the ends of periods). This detached manner of singing suits the quicker tempo of the groove, and the lilting feel of this faster pace also conditions her use of *vibrato*, a vocal technique she restricts primarily to longer notes at the end of phrases, where the broadening effect of a vibrating note, rather than inhibiting forward motion, delicately draws the passages to a close.

But Richard's choice of tempo does more than determine specific features of Karen's vocal style, for it eliminates the moment of stasis between the first and second verses, allowing the two verses to be joined together

Example 4. Disposition of the song's sections

	Richard Chamberlain	Dionne Warwick	Carpenters
	Length: 2:16 Tempo: *c.* 72 bpm	Length: 2:21 Tempo: *c.* 72 bpm	Length: 3:37 Tempo: *c.* 87 bpm
Intro			0:00　triplet piano riff 0:05　vibraphone added
Verse 1	0:00　electric guitar doubles voice; strings provide backdrop	0:00　cymbal splash opens recording; vibraphone doubles voice; strings provide backdrop	0:09　voice accompanied by pulsing piano chords in quarter notes
	0:05　*staccato* piano chords in eighth notes; bass, drums	0:04　pulsing piano chords in eighth notes; bass, drums	
	0:28　link to verse 2: arpeggio on piano, then guitar	0:25　link to verse 2: horn fill	

	Richard Chamberlain	Dionne Warwick	Carpenters
Verse 2	0:30 counter melody in strings added	0:29 counter melody in strings as in Chamberlain	0:31 strings, bass, drums added
	0:55 link to bridge: horn fill, strings emphasize dominant to tonic	0:55 link to bridge: horn fill, tympani roll	0:52 link to bridge: simple drum fill on the toms
Bridge	0:59 counter melody in strings; tension builds	0:59 counter melody in strings and backup singers; tension remains constant	0:55 subdued first statement; counter melody similar to Bacharach in woodwinds and strings; triplet eighth notes on muted cymbal; strings drop out for last two bars
	1:20 link to verse 3: two piano *glissandi*	1:21 link to verse 3: two piano *glissandi*	1:12 link to verse 3: two piano *glissandi*
Verse 3	1:24 accompaniment similar to verse 2	1:25 accompaniment similar to verse 2	1:15 accompaniment similar to verse 2 but backup singers echo Karen's phrases
	1:49 link to outro: horn fill	1:52 link to outro: horn fill	

(continued)

Example 4. (cont.)

	Richard Chamberlain	Dionne Warwick	Carpenters	
Outro	1:52 repetition of refrain; backup singers double Chamberlain			
		1:55 repetition of refrain; main melody in backup singers; Warwick echoes and decorates the tune		
Trumpet solo			1:36	abrupt modulation to D flat; trumpet imitates vocal phrasing
			1:49	refrain replaced by strings playing modified version of the opening piano figure
			1:57	link to bridge: new piano figuration accompanied by low-tuned toms
Bridge			1:59	double-tracked lead vocal followed by harmonic crescendo
			2:15	fills on toms lead to a cymbal roll that drives passage to a peak; tension then released across a one-second reverberant tail
Verse 3			2:19	arrangement similar to the first statement of verse 3
Ending 1			2:49	opening piano riff restated in A flat
Tag			3:00	vocal "wahs" on major ninth chords

seamlessly. At the beginning of the second verse, a thicker texture, achieved through the introduction of drums, bass, and strings, augments the intensity somewhat. Hal Blaine, the drummer on the recording, emphasizes the backbeat while tapping straight quarter notes on the hi-hat, and the bass guitar, reinforced by the kick drum, stresses the first and third beats of the bar. The strings, functioning as a backdrop to the metric interplay between the hi-hat and bass, provide chordal pads for the most part, but just before the refrain, a simple descending line in quarter notes fills the space in a manner reminiscent of the highly decorative melody Bacharach had composed for this purpose. Carpenter's transition to the bridge, similar to Bacharach's treatment of the passage, heightens tension only minimally, presumably because he wanted to save the most powerful approach to this section for the climactic moment of the recording, the repetition of the bridge. The first statement of the bridge, then, remains subdued, Carpenter simply adding woodwind instruments to a string figure he seems to have derived from Bacharach, while Blaine increases the rhythmic activity in the drums through a triplet eighth-note figure played on a muted cymbal. The strings drop out for the last two bars, and this leaves the woodwinds, bass, and drums to propel the instrumental backdrop subtly toward the two piano *glissandi* Herb Alpert insisted Carpenter retain from Bacharach's recording (Coleman 1994: 84). These clinching hooks, to borrow Alpert's words (ibid.), make an effective transition to the third verse, but Carpenter begins this verse somewhat differently from the previous two verses, for Hal Blaine employs low-tuned toms to cover the static nature of this compositional moment. The rest of the verse, however, proceeds in a manner similar to the second verse, except that Carpenter introduces backup singers who echo the phrases Karen sings.

At the end of the third verse, following a quarter second of silence, the music abruptly modulates to D flat and Chuck Findley, the trumpet solo-ist on the recording, plays the verse melody in imitation of Karen's style of phrasing (Coleman 1994: 84).[11] The disposition of the instrumental back-drop behind the trumpet remains similar to that of the previous verse, but at the end of the verse, Richard replaces the refrain with a section in which the strings play a modified version of the opening piano figure. The final bar of this passage brings the piano to the fore, and new keyboard figuration, accompanied by low-tuned toms, leads listeners to the height-ened intensity of the second bridge. Here, Richard's treatment of the vocal strengthens the impact of the section considerably, even though he main-tains much of the earlier instrumentation and part writing (especially the string and woodwind figures, along with triplet eighth-notes on the muted cymbal, the kick drum accentuating the first and third beats, and the hi-hat articulating the backbeat). He double tracks Karen's voice in the first line of text and then in the second line supports it with harmonies that widen from two to three to four notes to create a harmonic crescendo to the apex of the song. This carefully crafted intensification culminates in the last bar with Hal Blaine's drum work, where fills on the toms lead to a cymbal roll that drives the passage to a peak. The tension reached in this climactic moment is released across a one-second reverberant tail of cymbal and piano, and the sudden textural thinning that follows returns listeners to the emotional plane of the verses. Richard applies generous reverb to the two notes of the vocal pickup, both sung without accompaniment, but other than this, his arrangement for the repetition of the third verse retains much of its earlier flavor. The verse closes with two statements of the refrain, and a return of the opening piano riff in A flat rounds out the structure, "bookending" the song.

But because Richard did not want to end "Close to You" just as it had begun, he decided to compose a vocal tag that, in his words, "came out of left field." Inspired by the way Bacharach had concluded "Raindrops Keep Fallin' on My Head," he extended the song by thirty-eight seconds with vocal "wahs" based on rich harmonies involving major ninth chords alternating between D flat and A flat. The striking effect of the new material in this lush postlude became one of the most memorable sonic events of the song, so much so that Richard himself questions whether anyone could imagine "Close to You" ending without the tag. In fact, after hearing the Carpenters' version of the song, one can easily understand why Bacharach praised Richard and Karen for "nailing" it. Their long, nuanced structure, with its lilting groove and striking arrangement, captivated listeners and produced the Carpenters first number one record. The gold sales award the single received from the Recording Industry Association of America on August 12, 1970, three months after the record was released, attests to the wide appeal of the song.

Bacharach occasionally spoke about the popularity of his music, telling the *New Yorker* in 1968 that "the wild thing about my songs is that they cross the two age gaps. They're hits with people my parents' age and they're hits with the kids, too" (Ross 1968: 45), and at least one commentator from the late 1960s, Bob Shayne of the *Los Angeles Times*, noted Bacharach's unique ability to bridge the generation gap. Bacharach and David songs, Shayne observed, "especially when produced by them and sung by Dionne Warwick, get played on the middle-of-the-road radio stations, the rock stations, and most rhythm and blues stations as well. Their records are bought by whites and blacks, young and old" (1968: C7). Indeed, Hubert Saal, writing for *Newsweek* in 1970, noticed that Bacharach's audience at the Westbury Music Fair was a cross-section of people ranging in age from eight to eighty, and in his article, he quotes from a letter Bacharach received from a young Catholic school girl asking him to write a school yell for her: "What would take me two weeks will take you only five minutes . . . P.S. The nuns dig you too" (p. 50).

One of the factors contributing to Bacharach and David's wide appeal seems to have been their desire to please themselves instead of writing for a specific market. "When Hal and I write," Bacharach says, "we don't think about markets or what will go. Is this a comer? Is this too complicated for the people? No. I'm just trying to satisfy myself" (Shayne

1968: C7). By writing songs he liked, Bacharach believed that other people might like them, too, and the one thing he and David never did in their career was "try to write a 'commercial' song. [We] don't think in terms of hits. [We] think in terms of good and bad" ("Bacharach & David" 1978: 17). Commercial aspirations, Bacharach felt, would just trap them in a corner (Cumming 2001), and ironically one of their most "uncommercial" songs, the jazz waltz "Wives and Lovers," became a hit for Jack Jones in the USA.[12] A good record, then, at least according to Bacharach, David, and Richard Carpenter, needs not only the right artist but also the right showcase. Bacharach readily admits that with "Close to You" he and David found neither the appropriate artist or arrangement, but the Carpenters, in "nailing" the song, found a musical concept that produced a much more appealing expressive flow (Hilburn 1970: N37; DeMain 1997). As Bacharach said in 1970, shortly after the Carpenters released their version of "Close to You," "you write some music and think it has fallen dead . . . then all of a sudden the thing takes off" (Hebert 1970: D8).

As this case study demonstrates, the discovery of the precise combination of expressive elements that would create an appealing record can elude even the best recordists. Subtle alterations of the type Bacharach incorporated in his second recording of "(They Long to Be) Close to You" clearly missed the mark, and the song lay dormant until Richard Carpenter realized its full potential by placing Bacharach's text in a different setting. Similarly, The Who's first attempt at recording "Behind Blue Eyes" in New York failed to produce a version acceptable to the band, and it took the enhancements conceived in London to transform Townshend's original conception into a powerful musical discourse. Indeed, the search for effective verbal and musical arguments motivated many recordists in the 1960s to craft their aural landscapes from interpretive strategies that would help turn songs into hits instead of misses.

Notes

INTRODUCTION

1 I use the words pop and rock interchangeably as generic terms for the various musical styles encompassed by Top 40 charts in the 1960s.

CHAPTER 1

1 Webb uses the phrase "spans of meaning" to refer to individual lines of text, whereas I employ it to describe a paragraph of thought.

2 Both Sheila Davis (1985: 93) and Jimmy Webb (1998: 42–43, 91–94) discuss the conversational nature of pop lyrics, Webb commenting on the positive effect casual speech, without impeccable grammar, can make.

3 For further discussion of this figure as employed in early seventeenth-century music, see Toft (1993: 26–29).

4 For further discussion of this figure, see Toft (1993: 25–26).

5 For further discussion of this figure, see Sonnino (1968: 24–25).

6 For further discussion of this figure, see Toft (1993: 25, 133–34, 152–53).

7 This diagram is based on graphs that Jimmy Webb (1998: 105–28) employs to illustrate emotional line.

CHAPTER 2

1 For a discussion of this principle in relation to recitative, see Toft (2000: 3).
2 When the song was written, the introductory vocal section would have been called a "verse" and the remainder of the song would have been designated a "chorus," but in order to avoid confusion between the nomenclature of the 1930s and the terminology I employed in the previous chapter, I prefer to call the "verse" an introductory section and to subdivide the "chorus" into three verses and a bridge.
3 For further discussion of the differences between interpretation and re-creation, see Potter (1998: 167–68) and Toft (2004: 368–71).
4 Appoggiaturas are discussed more fully in Chapter 4.

CHAPTER 3

1 See, for example, The Yardbirds' "For Your Love" which travels up the neck from a first-position Em chord to barré chords on G, A, and Am. These types of chord progressions distinguish the harmonic idiom of pop/rock in the 1960s from traditional harmonic practices, particularly with regard to the parallel motion of barré chords played in succession and the cross-relations embodied in the movement from C to A, F to D, and G to E. At least one other scholar, Ken Stephenson, has acknowledged the emergence of new practices in the 1960s, and he describes the pervasiveness of this non-traditional harmonic style as a "new standard" (2002: 101).
2 "I Think We're Alone Now":
A E D A | A C♯m F♯m E | C♯m A G E

"Hurdy Gurdy Man":
F C G | G Bm C D

"Words":
G A D C G B♭ F G A D | D G D G

"(Sittin' on) the Dock of the Bay":
G B C B B♭ A | G E G E G A G E | G D C F D

"Lay Lady Lay":
A C♯m G Bm | E F♯m A | C♯m E A C♯m Bm A

3 See, in particular, the collections of essays published in Covach and Boone (1997) and Everett (2000b), as well as Bobbitt (1976), Burns (2005), Everett (1999, 2001a, 2004), and Stephenson (2002).

4 See Tagg (2003: 13–14) for a discussion of why barré-chord progressions, so common in guitar-based popular music, "function in a radically different way to progressions in the idiom of classical harmony."

5 Curiously, although the chord built on the sixth degree of the scale (E) is major, the B chord is labeled as V/vi (i.e. the sixth step of the scale is identified as a minor chord). The E chord is then labeled as V/ii, even though an A major chord has already sounded on the second degree of the scale. Throughout his chapter on "Harmonic Succession," Stephenson applies principles and labels from common-practice tonality, even though at the beginning of the chapter he argues that a new practice with "its own set of harmonic conventions" had emerged in the 1960s (2002: 101).

6 The guitarist actually plays a Bm chord, not a II⁷. Bob Dylan does, however, sing the pitch "a" above the chord, and Everett's label takes the vocal pitch into consideration.

7 Allan Moore (1995: 185–88) draws a similar conclusion and outlines some of the problems associated with applying Schenkerian analysis to rock music. Richard Middleton (2000: 1–19), among others (for example, Walser 2000), also takes issue with formalist analysis, and for an impassioned response to Middleton's critique, see Everett (2001b). Despite adverse commentary, Everett remains convinced of the superiority of the Schenkerian technique: "It is my belief that a Schenkerian understanding of tonal relationships allows for a clearer hearing of the variations among rock's tonal approaches than what has been afforded by methods thus far appearing in other analyses" (2004: par. 2, n. 2). Moreover, it is Everett's contention "(supported by a close study of more than 6,000 popular songs produced in the 1950s and 60s) that the tonal norms basic to the pop music from which rock emerged are the same norms common to the system of common-practice tonality. These norms are still adhered to, in varying degrees, in most current popular music, although we also find today many competing approaches to 'normal' tonality" (2004: par. 3).

8 Allan Moore (1992; 1995: esp. 185–88; 2001: esp. 52–55) also discusses popular music from a modal perspective, and although he does not link modal features directly to guitar playing, he makes a strong case for the application of modal theory to the harmony of rock music. Similarly, Richard Middleton (1990: esp. 195, 198–99) comments upon the importance of modality in rock music, and Alf Björnberg (1989) and Robert Walser (1993: 46–48, 52–53, 127, 156) treat modal harmony in contemporary popular music and heavy-metal music. Chris McDonald (2000) explores modal subversion in alternative music, and Stan Hawkins (2002: 108–09) discusses modality in Annie Lennox's "Money Can't Buy It."

9 For a detailed discussion of these non-harmonic relations in sixteenth-century music, see Toft (1992: 7–163, passim). My theory of modality clearly differs from the ones expounded by Philip Tagg (2003: 14–17), who restricts major triads to specific steps of a modal scale and invokes a theory of alteration (through *tierce de Picardie*) to explain the presence of major chords on other scale degrees, and Chris McDonald (2000), who not only describes scales as having major or minor modality but also refers to modes as being subverted by cross-relations. Similarly, my approach differs from that of Alf Björnberg (1989), Stan Hawkins (2002: 108–09), Allan F. Moore (1995), and Robert Walser (1993: 46–48, 52–53, 127, 156), for they mix modal principles with tonal labels in their work.

10 The highest chart positions for the five songs are:

	UK	USA	
"(Sittin' on the) Dock of the Bay" (1968)	3	1	
"Lay Lady Lay" (1969)	5	7	
"I Think We're Alone Now" (1967)	—	4	(not released in the UK)
"Hurdy Gurdy Man" (1968)	4	5	
"Words" (1968)	8	15	

Information taken from Davies (1998), Strong (2000), and Whitburn (2000).

11 Music theorists tend to view the falling fifth as a clear indication of tonality, but falling fifths are no more indicative of tonality in the popular music I discuss here than they are in Renaissance modal music, where their presence has been taken as a sign of incipient tonality (see, for example, Lowinsky 1961: 4). While motion by a fifth is an important stabilizing factor in tonality,

it does not have such a dramatic effect in modal systems. In the late fifteenth and sixteenth centuries, for example, strong cadences were created by two voices moving by step to a resting point, and the falling fifth usually occurred as a by-product of the other contrapuntal lines working independently of the two voices controlling the cadence. Don M. Randel discussed this facet of modality in 1971 and distinguished modal cadential motion from that of triadic tonality (see esp. 77–79).

12 This pattern also appears in "(Sittin' on) the Dock of the Bay."

13 Everett (2000a: 323–26; 2004: par. 11) describes progressions like the one in "Hurdy Gurdy Man" as double-plagal cadences (♭VII–IV–I) and argues that they do not have a modal basis because they are chromatic events, involving notes from outside the tonal scale, that create a "counterpoint of continual downward-resolving neighbors" (he views IV as a neighbor to I, an embellishment without harmonic function; see 2000a: 323). One of the advantages of a modal theoretical system, however, is that it eliminates the need for describing the seventh step of the scale as ♭VII. As Allan Moore (1995) has pointed out, the problem with the concept of the flattened seventh is that it presupposes that raised sevenths are the norm in rock music when clearly, for a great deal of popular music, they are not. Moreover, in modal systems there is no need to think of any scale degree as a flattened note. For example, Robert Walser (1993: 156) classifies the Aeolian mode progression C–D–E as ♭VI–♭VII–I, even though the sixth and seventh steps of the E-Aeolian scale are normally C and D. His use of flat signs assumes that C♯ and D♯ are part of this mode, when they are not, for a ♭VI chord in E-Aeolian would actually be C♭ and a ♭VII chord, D♭.

14 The Arabic numbers indicate the step of the scale upon which a chord is built. They do not designate function within the modal system.

CHAPTER 4

1 I have reconstructed many of the older practices in Toft (2000) and that study provides the basis for the discussion of the vocal techniques treated in this chapter. However, without recordings to document the precise ways in which singers from the late eighteenth and early nineteenth centuries applied the principles of *bel canto* to specific works, all reconstructions of performance practices pre-dating the advent of sound recording must remain speculative.

2 Richard Middleton (1993: 187) first pointed this out.

3 I explode many of the myths surrounding *bel canto* in Toft (2000), and in Toft (2004) I explore one aspect of the similarities between *bel canto* and modern popular/jazz singing, that is, grammatical and rhetorical phrasing.

4 Pausing and *bel canto* phrasing have been discussed extensively in Toft (2000; 2004).

5 The comments cited here conflate García (1857: 56) and García (1847: pt. 2, 35–36; trans. pt. 2, 103).

6 The complexities of *legato* and *staccato* are discussed at length in Toft (2000: 58–68).

7 For further information, see Toft (2000: 66).

8 On Bacharach's penchant for notational precision and his insistence that the singers he produced perform exactly what he had written, see Chapter 7.

9 See, for example, writers as diverse as Corri (1810: 3–4) and Novello (1856: 15–16).

10 For a fuller discussion of register and tonal qualities of the voice, see Toft (2000: 23–30).

11 On this aspect of the old *bel canto* style, see Corri (1810: 67), Gardiner (1832: 145), and Addison (?1850: 11).

12 On this female "falsetto stop," see the comments on Giuditta Pasta and Henriette Sontag in *New Monthly Magazine* (1828: 203).

13 See Toft (2000: 30–36) for a fuller discussion of *vibrato* in the *bel canto* era.

CHAPTER 5

1 For a detailed study of the collaborative activities of recordists, see Zak (2001).

2 On the composition of "Laughing," see Einarson and Bachman (2000: 159–60), and on Bachman's approach to teaching songwriting, see ibid. p. 317.

3 For a survey of rhetoric in classical times, see Corbett (1990). Corbett addresses the purpose of rhetoric on pp. 20–22.

4 The following discussion of invention and arrangement is based mainly on Aristotle, *On Rhetoric*; Cicero, *De Inventione*; Cicero, *De Oratore*; Cicero, *Topica*; *Rhetorica ad Herennium*; and Quintilian, *Institutio Oratoria*. Many of the pertinent sections from these texts have been published in English translation in Benson and Prosser (1972). Convenient summaries of the

central tenets of invention and arrangement are found in Lanham (1968: 106–16) and Enos (1996: 32–36, 349–55, 698–703, 724–26).

5 Examples of the various kinds of *topoi* may be found in Lanham (1968: 107–12).

6 On this aspect of Ramée's theory of rhetoric, see Howell (1961: 160–65).

7 *Exordium* may be defined as "the beginning whose purpose is to prepare the audience to listen with interest" (Sonnino 1968: 243).

8 The notion of "sonic presence" is discussed in Zak (2001: 45–47).

CHAPTER 6

1 For detailed chronicles of the *Lifehouse* saga, see Atkins (2000: 139–76) and Wilkerson (2008: 146–75, 475–82).

2 John Atkins (2000: 147) has noted that of the songs Townshend had written for the project, only two, "Getting in Tune" and "Pure and Easy," actually captured "the central essence" of the *Lifehouse* story, the "idea of music as a source of social and spiritual power." The others simply reflect pertinent aspects of Townshend's theme.

CHAPTER 7

1 See, for example, Burt Bacharach's comments in Ross (1968: 45): "No matter how groovy the electronic devices are these days, there's got to be a song. Electronic devices are marvellous. But nobody's going to whistle electronic devices. You've got to have a song." Albin Zak (2007) has discussed the prevalence of this attitude in the music industry.

2 Various writers note Bacharach's lack of success with the song (see, for example, Platts [2003: 76–77]), but Serene Dominic (2003: 110–11) relegates Bacharach's first two productions to the dustbins of the 1960s, describing the song as coming "very close to becoming a throwaway despite having a lot going for it."

3 In a similar fashion, Lloyd Whitesell (2008: 3–4) rummages through Joni Mitchell's "musical toolkit (her 'box of paints,' as she might put it) to establish a basis for judgments about the quality of her songwriting."

4 See also his opinion on other songs in "Bacharach & David" (1978: 14–15); Platts (2003: 56–57); and Zollo (2003: 208).

5 In an interview with Paul Zollo (2003: 211), David said that he "wrote ['Close to You'] to the music."

6 David spoke of his desire for natural, unpretentious vocabulary in his songs to Digby Diehl (1970: C15). In relation to David's lyrics for "The Windows of the World," Dionne Warwick commented to interviewer Robin Platts: "he tells [a story] simply in just the way we'd like to say it ourselves" (1997: 51).

7 See also Phil Ramone's comments in DeMain (1997): "Oh yeah [most of the recordings were done live]. Both the studios at A&R that they [Bacharach and David] used had some kind of isolation for the vocals, because we separated the group from Dionne, but they were right in the room. There was not much overdubbing in those days."

8 On the autonomy granted to Bacharach by Scepter Records, the label for which he recorded during the period under consideration, see Brocken (2003: 126) and Platts (2003: 25), and on Bacharach's dissatisfaction with other people's productions of his songs, see "Bacharach & David" (1978: 8); Ross (1968: 46); Shayne (1968: C7); Saal (1970: 51); Sutherland (1986: 24); and Zollo (2003: 208).

9 On this aspect of Bacharach's style of working, see the comments of various musicians cited in Saal (1970: 52); Brocken (2003: 135); and Platts (2003: 49–50), as well as Bacharach's acknowledgement quoted in DiMartino (1998): "I'm not as hard on myself as I used to be — I'm hard on myself — maybe it's become a recognition that I'm gonna get as close to 100 per cent as I can."

10 See, for example, the particularly caustic comments in Dominic (2003: 110): "Bacharach's strident piano arrangement gives Chamberlain little choice but to robotically follow every chord change."

11 Trumpeters often conceived their phrasing in terms of vocal lines, and in his own work, Bacharach regularly wrote words under the notes of an instrumental line. He related his reasons for this practice to Bill DeMain (1997): "I've always been a big believer in words with notes. I used to write for the trumpet players, or the reed players, anybody that would have a singular statement to make on a record, I'd write the lyric underneath. So they'd be playing melody notation but they'd try to speak through their instrument the actual lyric. . . . There was a reason I did it. There are certain things that can't really be notated, I find in an orchestration. It's maybe two eighth notes, a sixteenth note and another eighth note and that's the way it should be notated, but that's not the way it totally feels. But if you put words with it, or even vowel sounds, it does make a difference."

12 See David's comments on this song in Rudman (1964b: 18): "as we saw it,

the only honest approach was to do it off-beat musically. So we wrote it as a jazz waltz which you will admit is very unlikely for commercial aspirations . . . The sophisticated lyric I wrote obviously was not designed for teen-age appeal."

Bibliography

Addison, John. ?1850. *Singing, Practically Treated in a Series of Instructions*. London: D'Almaine.

Aristotle. 1991. *On Rhetoric*, trans. George A. Kennedy. New York: Oxford University Press.

Atkins, John. 2000. *The Who on Record: A Critical History, 1963–1998*. Jefferson, NC: McFarland.

——. 2003. "Who's Next and the Lifehouse Project." Liner notes to *Who's Next (Deluxe Edition)*. MCA Records, 088 113 056–2, pp. 11–21.

"Bacharach & David". 1978. Unpaginated introduction to the songbook *Bacharach & David*. Hollywood: Almo Publications.

Bacon, Richard M. 1966. *Elements of Vocal Science*, ed. Edward Foreman. Champaign, IL: Pro Musica Press. (First published in 1824, London: Baldwin, Cradock & Joy).

Benson, Thomas W. and Michael H. Prosser. 1972. *Readings in Classical Rhetoric*. Bloomington, IN: Indiana University Press.

Björnberg, Alf. 1989. "On Aeolian Harmony in Contemporary
Popular Music," Göteborg: IASPM — Nordic Branch Working
Papers, no. DK 1. In Allan F. Moore, ed., *Critical Essays in Popular
Musicology*, pp. 275–82. Aldershot: Ashgate, 2007.

Blum, Stephen. 1992. "Analysis of Musical Style." In Helen Myers, ed.,
Ethnomusicology: An Introduction, pp. 165–218. New York: W. W.
Norton.

Bobbitt, Richard. 1976. *Harmonic Technique in the Rock Idiom*.
Belmont, CA: Wadsworth.

Boone, Graeme M. 1997. "Tonal and Expressive Ambiguity in 'Dark
Star.'" In John Covach and Graeme M. Boone, eds., *Understanding
Rock: Essays in Musical Analysis*, pp. 171–210. New York: Oxford
University Press.

Bowman, Rob. 2003. "The Determining Role of Performance in the
Articulation of Meaning: The Case of 'Try a Little Tenderness.'"
In Allan F. Moore, ed., *Analyzing Popular Music*, pp. 103–30.
Cambridge: Cambridge University Press.

Breare, William. 1904. *Vocalism: Its Structure and Culture from an
English Standpoint*. London: G. P. Putnam's Sons.

Brocken, Michael. 2003. *Bacharach: Maestro! The Life of a Pop Genius*.
New Malden, UK: Chrome Dreams.

Brown, Matthew. 1997. "'Little Wing': A Study in Musical Cognition."
In John Covach and Graeme M. Boone, eds., *Understanding Rock:
Essays in Musical Analysis*, pp. 155–69. New York: Oxford University
Press.

Burns, Lori. 2000. "Analytic Methodologies for Rock Music: Harmonic
and Voice-Leading Strategies in Tori Amos's 'Crucify.'" In Walter
Everett, ed., *Expression in Pop-Rock Music: A Collection of Critical
and Analytical Essays*, pp. 213–46. New York: Garland Publishing.

——. 2005. "Meaning in a Popular Song: The Representation of
Masochistic Desire in Sarah McLachlan's 'Ice.'" In Deborah Stein, ed.,

Engaging Music: Essays in Music Analysis, pp. 136–48. New York: Oxford University Press.

Carpenter, Richard. "Carpenters Fans Ask . . . Richard Answers." Available at: http://www.richardandkarencarpenter.com/fans_ask_8. htm (accessed September 12, 2008).

Cicero. 1948. *De Oratore*. London: William Heinemann.

———. 1949a. *De Inventione*. London: William Heinemann.

———. 1949b. *Topica*. London: William Heinemann.

Cockin, William. 1775. *The Art of Delivering Written Language*. London: J. Dodsley. Reprint, Menston: Scolar Press, 1969.

Coleman, Ray. 1994. *The Carpenters: The Untold Story, an Authorized Biography*. New York: HarperCollins.

Corbett, Edward P. J. 1990. *Classical Rhetoric for the Modern Student*, 3rd ed. New York: Oxford University Press.

Corri, Domenico. 1810. *The Singer's Preceptor*. London: Longman, Hurst, Rees & Orme.

Covach, John. 1997. "We Won't Get Fooled Again: Rock Music and Musical Analysis." In David Schwarz, Anahid Kassabian, and Lawrence Siegel, eds., *Keeping Score: Music, Disciplinarity, Culture*, pp. 75–89. Charlottesville, VA: University Press of Virginia.

Covach, John and Graeme M. Boone, eds. 1997. *Understanding Rock: Essays in Musical Analysis*. New York: Oxford University Press.

Cumming, Alec. 2001. "There's Always Something There to Remind Me: The Burt Bacharach Story." Liner notes to *The Look of Love: The Burt Bacharach Collection*. Warner Music Canada, WTVD 88384.

Cunningham, Mark. 1998. *Good Vibrations: A History of Record Production*. London: Sanctuary Publishing.

David, Hal. "Words from Hal David." Available at: http://www.haldavid.com/words.htm (accessed August 20, 2008).

Davies, Chris. 1998. *British and American Hit Singles: 51 Years of Transatlantic Hits 1946–1997*. London: B. T. Batsford.

Davis, Sheila. 1985. *The Craft of Lyric Writing*. Cincinnati: Writer's Digest Books.

———. 1992. *The Songwriters Idea Book*. Cincinnati: Writer's Digest Books.

DeMain, Bill. 1997. "What's It All About, Bacharach?" *Switch*, June 1997. Available at: http://www.rocksbackpages.com (accessed September 28, 2008).

Diehl, Digby. 1970. "Hal David . . . Poet in Tempo." *Los Angeles Times*, December 31, 1970: C15.

DiMartino, Dave. 1998. "Elvis Costello with Burt Bacharach: *Painted from Memory*." *Mojo*, October 1998. Available at: http://www.rocks backpages.com (accessed September 30, 2008).

Dominic, Serene. 2003. *Burt Bacharach Song by Song*. New York: Schirmer Trade Books.

Egestorf, G. H. ?1815. *A Practical Dissertation on the Science of Singing*. London: (s.n.).

Einarson, John and Randy Bachman. 2000. *Randy Bachman: Takin' Care of Business*. Toronto: McArthur & Co.

Enos, Theresa, ed. 1996. *Encyclopedia of Rhetoric and Composition*. New York: Garland Publishing.

Everett, Walter. 1999. *The Beatles as Musicians:* Revolver *through the* Anthology. New York: Oxford University Press.

———. 2000a. "Confessions from Blueberry Hell, or, Pitch Can Be a Sticky Substance." In Walter Everett, ed., *Expression in Pop-Rock Music: A Collection of Critical and Analytical Essays*, 269–345. New York: Garland Publishing.

———. 2001a. *The Beatles as Musicians: The Quarry Men through* Rubber Soul. New York: Oxford University Press.

———. 2001b. "Review of Richard Middleton, ed., *Reading Pop: Approaches to Textual Analysis in Popular Music* (Oxford: Oxford University Press, 2000)." *Music Theory Online* 7. Available at: http://

mto.societymusictheory.org/issues/mto.01.7.6/mto.01.7.6.everett.
html (accessed June 15, 2007).

———. 2004. "Making Sense of Rock's Tonal Systems." *Music Theory
Online* 10. Available at: http://mto.societymusictheory.org/issues/
mto.04.10.4/mto.04.10.4.w_everett.html (accessed July 6, 2007).

Everett, Walter, ed. 2000b. *Expression in Pop-Rock Music: A Collection
of Critical and Analytical Essays.* New York: Garland Publishing.

García, Manuel. 1857. *New Treatise on the Art of Singing.* London:
Cramer, Beale & Chappell.

———. 1847. *Traité complet de l'art du chant*, Paris: Chez l'auteur.
Reprint, Geneva: Minkoff, 1985. Trans. Donald V. Paschke, *A
Complete Treatise on the Art of Singing.* New York: Da Capo, 1975
[part 2] and 1984 [part 1].

Gardiner, William. 1832. *The Music of Nature.* London: Longman, Rees,
Orme, Brown, Green & Longman.

Gracyk, Theodore. 1996. *Rhythm and Noise: An Aesthetics of Rock.*
Durham, NC: Duke University Press.

Hamilton, James Alexander. 1853. *Modern Instructions in Singing.*
London: Robert Cocks.

Harrison, Daniel. 1997. "After Sundown: The Beach Boys' Experimental
Music." In John Covach and Graeme M. Boone, eds., *Understanding
Rock: Essays in Musical Analysis*, pp. 33–57. New York: Oxford
University Press.

Hawkins, Stan. 2002. *Settling the Pop Score: Pop Texts and Identity
Politics.* Aldershot: Ashgate.

Headlam, Dave. 1997. "Blues Transformations in the Music of Cream."
In John Covach and Graeme M. Boone, eds., *Understanding Rock:
Essays in Musical Analysis*, pp. 59–92. New York: Oxford University
Press.

Hebert, Bob. 1970. "Bacharach — He's Had Winners in Music, but Few
in Racing." *Los Angeles Times*, July 6, 1970: D8.

Hilburn, Robert. 1970. "Bacharach Weighs His Future." *Los Angeles Times*, July 5, 1970: N37.

Howell, Wilbur Samuel. 1961. *Logic and Rhetoric in England, 1500–1700*. New York: Russell & Russell.

Kitchiner, William. 1821. *Observations on Vocal Music*. London: Hurst, Robinson.

Krims, Adam. 2000. *Rap Music and the Poetics of Identity*. Cambridge: Cambridge University Press.

Lanham, Richard A. 1968. *A Handlist of Rhetorical Terms*. Berkeley, CA: University of California Press.

Lanza, Gesualdo. ?1820. *Elements of Singing*. London: Chappell.

Lowinsky, Edward. 1961. *Tonality and Atonality in Sixteenth-Century Music*. Berkeley, CA: University of California Press.

McDonald, Chris. 2000. "Exploring Modal Subversions in Alternative Music." *Popular Music* 19: 355–63.

Middleton, Richard. 1990. *Studying Popular Music*. Milton Keynes: Open University Press.

———. 1993. "Popular Music Analysis and Musicology: Bridging the Gap." *Popular Music* 12: 177–90.

Middleton, Richard, ed. 2000. *Reading Pop: Approaches to Textual Analysis in Popular Music*. Oxford: Oxford University Press.

Miles, Barry. 1997. *Paul McCartney: Many Years from Now*. New York: H. Holt.

Moore, Allan F. 1992. "Patterns of Harmony." *Popular Music* 11: 73–106.

———. 1995. "The So-Called 'Flattened Seventh' in Rock." *Popular Music* 14: 185–201.

———. 2001. *Rock: The Primary Text*, 2nd ed. Aldershot: Ashgate.

Moore, Allan F., ed. 2003. *Analyzing Popular Music*. Cambridge: Cambridge University Press.

———. 2007. *Critical Essays in Popular Musicology*. Aldershot: Ashgate.

Nathan, Isaac. 1836. *Musurgia Vocalis*. London: Fentum.

Neill, Andy and Matt Kent. 2002. *Anyway Anyhow Anywhere: The Complete Chronicle of The Who 1958–1978*. London: Virgin Books.

New Monthly Magazine 24: May 1828.

Novello, Mary. 1856. *Voice and Vocal Art*, 2nd ed. London: J. Alfred Novello.

O'Brien, Lucy. 2002. *She Bop II: The Definitive History of Women in Rock, Pop and Soul*. New York: Continuum.

Olsen, Eric, Paul Verna, and Carlo Wolff. 1999. "Richard Carpenter." In *The Encyclopedia of Record Producers*, pp. 114–15. New York: Watson-Guptill Publications.

Peacham, Henry. 1593. *The Garden of Eloquence*. London: H. Jackson. Reprint, Gainesville, FL: Scholars' Facsimiles & Reprints, 1954.

Philipps, Thomas. 1826. *Elementary Principles and Practices for Singing*. Dublin: J. Willis.

Platts, Robin. 1997. "Anyone Who Had a Heart: The Songs of Burt Bacharach and Hal David." *Discoveries*, December 1997: 48–54.

———. 2003. *Burt Bacharach and Hal David: What the World Needs Now*. Burlington, ON: Collector's Guide Publishing.

Potter, John. 1998. *Vocal Authority: Singing Style and Ideology*. Cambridge: Cambridge University Press.

Quintilian. 1953–61. *Institutio Oratoria*, 4 vols. London: William Heinemann.

Ramée, Pierre de la. 1555. *Dialectique*. Paris: André Wechel. Michel Dassonville, ed., Geneva: Librairie Droz, 1964.

Randel, Don. 1971. "Emerging Triadic Tonality in the Fifteenth Century." *Musical Quarterly* 57: 73–86.

Rhetorica ad Herennium. 1954. London: William Heinemann.

Robertson, Joseph. 1785. *An Essay on Punctuation*. London: J. Walter. Reprint, Menston: Scolar Press, 1969.

Ross, Lillian. 1968. "Hits." *New Yorker* 14, September 1968: 44–47.

Rudman, Kal. 1964a. "David & Bachrach [*sic*] Profile: Part 1." *Billboard* August 8, 1964: 14.

———. 1964b. "David & Bachrach [*sic*] Profile: Part 2." *Billboard* August 15, 1964: 18.

Saal, Hubert. 1966. "Gospel Girl." *Newsweek*, October 10, 1966: 101–02.

———. 1970. "Burt Bacharach the Music Man 1970." *Newsweek*, June 22, 1970: 50–54.

Shayne, Bob. 1968. "Broadway Score Promises New Spot for Bacharach." *Los Angeles Times*, September 1, 1968: C7.

Sonnino, Lee A. 1968. *A Handbook to Sixteenth-Century Rhetoric*. London: Routledge & Kegan Paul.

Stephenson, Ken. 2002. *What to Listen for in Rock: A Stylistic Analysis*. New Haven, CT: Yale University Press.

Strong, Martin C. 2000. *The Great Rock Discography*, 5th ed. Edinburgh: Mojo Books.

Sutherland, Sam. 1986. "Bacharach and Sager Set Sights on Producing." *Billboard*, August 16, 1986: 24–25.

Tagg, Philip. 2003. "Tagg's Harmony Handout or 'Definitions of Terms to do with Tonal Polyphony.'" Available at: http://tagg.org/texts.html (accessed June 25, 2007).

Toft, Robert. 1992. *Aural Images of Lost Traditions: Sharps and Flats in the Sixteenth Century*. Toronto: University of Toronto Press.

———. 1993. *Tune Thy Musicke to Thy Hart: The Art of Eloquent Singing in England, 1597–1622*. Toronto: University of Toronto Press.

———. 2000. *Heart to Heart: Expressive Singing in England 1780–1830*. Oxford: Oxford University Press.

———. 2004. "Rendering the Sense More Conspicuous: Grammatical and Rhetorical Principles of Vocal Phrasing in Art and Popular/Jazz Music." *Music & Letters* 85: 368–87.

Townshend, Pete. 2000. Liner notes to *Scoop*. Eel Pie Recording Productions.

———. 2003. "Who's Next." Liner notes to *Who's Next* (*Deluxe Edition*). MCA Records, 088 113 056-2, pp. 3–9.

Turner, John. 1833. *A Manual of Instruction in Vocal Music*. London: John W. Parker. Reprint, Kilkenny: Boethius Press, 1983.

Wagner, Naphtali. 2002. "Tonal Family Resemblance in *Revolver*." In Russell Reising, ed., *Every Sound There Is: The Beatles'* Revolver *and the Transformation of Rock and Roll*, pp. 109–20. Aldershot: Ashgate.

Wainewright, Harriett. 1836. *Critical Remarks on the Art of Singing*. London: T. and J. Hoitt.

Walser, Robert. 1993. *Running with the Devil: Power, Gender, and Madness in Heavy Metal Music*. Hanover, NH: Wesleyan University Press.

———. 2000. "Review of *Understanding Rock: Essays in Musical Analysis*, ed. John Covach, Graeme M. Boone (New York: Oxford University Press, 1997)." *Notes* 57: 355–57.

———. 2003. "Popular Music Analysis: Ten Apothegms and Four Instances." In Allan F. Moore, ed., *Analyzing Popular Music*, pp. 16–38. Cambridge: Cambridge University Press.

Webb, Jimmy. 1998. *Tunesmith: Inside the Art of Songwriting*. New York: Hyperion.

Whitburn, Joel. 2000. *The Billboard Book of Top 40 Hits*, 7th ed. New York: Billboard Books.

Whitesell, Lloyd. 2008. *The Music of Joni Mitchell*. New York: Oxford University Press.

Wilkerson, Mark. 2008. *Who Are You: The Life of Pete Townshend*. London: Omnibus Press.

Wilson, John S. 1968. "Loyalty Is a Girl Named Dionne." *New York Times*, May 12, 1968: D17.

Wilson, Thomas. 1553. *Arte of Rhetorique*. London: Richard Grafton. Thomas J. Derrick, ed. New York: Garland Publishing, 1982.

Wood, Harry, Jimmy Campbell, and Reg Connelly. 1933. "Try a Little Tenderness." New York: Robbins Music Corporation.

Zak, Albin J. 2001. *The Poetics of Rock: Cutting Tracks, Making Records*. Berkeley, CA: University of California Press.

——. 2007. "Editorial." *Journal of the Art of Record Production* 1/ii. Available at: http://www.artofrecordproduction.com (accessed August 12, 2008).

Zollo, Paul. 2003. *Songwriters on Songwriting*. Cambridge, MA: Da Capo Press.

Discography

The 5th Dimension. 1970. "One Less Bell to Answer," *The Look of Love, The Burt Bacharach Collection*. Warner Music Canada, WTVD 88384, 2001.

Alpert, Herb and the Tijuana Brass. 1968. "This Guy's in Love with You," *The Look of Love, The Burt Bacharach Collection*. Warner Music Canada, WTVD 88384, 2001.

The Beach Boys. 1964. "Don't Worry Baby," *The Very Best of the Beach Boys, Sounds of Summer*. Capitol/EMI, 72435-82710-2-7, 2003.

The Beatles. 1965. "Ticket to Ride," *Help!* EMI Parlophone, C2 46439, n.d.

———. 1966. "Here, There, and Everywhere," *Revolver*. EMI Parlophone, C2 0 7777 46441 2 9, n.d.

Bee Gees. 1967. "New York Mining Disaster 1941," *Best of Bee Gees*, vol. 1. Polydor, 831 594-2, n.d.

———. 1968. "Words," *Best of Bee Gees*, vol. 1. Polydor, 831 594-2, n.d.

Blood, Sweat & Tears. 1970. "Hi-De-Ho That Old Sweet Roll," *Greatest Hits*. Columbia/Legacy, CK 65729, 1999.

The Buckinghams. 1967. "Kind of a Drag," *Mercy, Mercy, Mercy (A Collection)*. Columbia/Legacy, CK 47718, 1991.

Campbell, Glen. 1967. "By the Time I Get to Phoenix," *All-Time Favorite Hits*. EMI Cema Special Markets, S21 57396, 1991.

Carpenters. 1969. "Ticket to Ride," *Carpenters: The Singles*. A&M, CD-3601, n.d.

———. 1970a. "Close to You," *Carpenters: The Singles*. A&M, CD-3601, n.d.

———. 1970b. "We've Only Just Begun," *Carpenters: The Singles*. A&M, CD-3601, n.d.

Chamberlain, Richard. 1963. "They Long to Be Close to You." MGM, K13170.

Como, Perry. 1958. "Magic Moments," *The Look of Love, The Burt Bacharach Collection*. Warner Music Canada, WTVD 88384, 2001.

Cooke, Sam. 1964. "Try a Little Tenderness," *Sam Cooke at the Copa*. Abkco Records, 99702, 2003.

Crosby, Bing. 1933. "Try a Little Tenderness," *Some of These Days, Classic Crosby, Vol. 2*. Naxos, 8.120562, 2001.

———. 1955. "Try a Little Tenderness," *Anything Goes, The Best of Bing Crosby*. Kaz Records/Pulse, PDS CD 532, 1996.

The Dave Clark Five. 1964a. "Because," *The Hits*. Dave Clark Productions/Universal Music, 1781774, 2008.

———. 1964b. "Do You Love Me," *The Hits*. Dave Clark Productions/Universal Music, 1781774, 2008.

Donovan. 1968. "Hurdy Gurdy Man," *Donovan's Greatist Hits*. Epic, EK 65730, 1999.

Dylan, Bob. 1965. "Positively 4th Street," *Bob Dylan's Greatest Hits*. Columbia, CK 65975, 1999.

———. 1969. "Lay Lady Lay," *Nashville Skyline*. Columbia, WCK-9825, n.d.

Etting, Ruth. 1933. "Try a Little Tenderness," *Let Me Call You Sweetheart*. Take Two Records, TT 224, 1987.

Franklin, Aretha. 1962. "Try a Little Tenderness," *The Tender, The Moving, The Swinging Aretha Franklin*. In *Two Classic Albums from Aretha Franklin*. Columbia, 516019 2, 2004.

Gentry, Bobbie. 1967. "Ode to Billie Joe," *Billboard Top Pop Hits, 1967*. Rhino Records, R2 71937, 1995.

The Guess Who. 1969. "Laughing," *The Guess Who: The Ultimate Collection*. BMG Entertainment, RCA 07063 67300-2, 1997.

James, Tommy and the Shondells. 1967. "I Think We're Alone Now," *Anthology*. Rhino Records, R2 70920, 1989.

The Jimi Hendrix Experience. 1967a. "Hey Joe," *Are You Experienced*. MCA Records, MCASD-11602, 1997.

———. 1967b. "The Wind Cries Mary," *Are You Experienced*. MCA Records, MCASD-11602, 1997.

Jones, Tom. 1965. "It's Not Unusual," *Tom Jones, Englebert Humperdinck, Their Greatest Hits*. Universal Music, 314 520 243-2, 2001.

Led Zeppelin. 1971. "Stairway to Heaven," *Led Zeppelin IV*. Atlantic, CD 82638, n.d.

Lewis, Ted. 1933. "Try a Little Tenderness," *Ted Lewis & His Band 1929–1934*. Timeless Records, CBC1074, 2003.

Mitchell, Joni. 1969. "Both Sides, Now," *Clouds*. Reprise, CD 6341, n.d.

The Monkees. 1967a. "I'm a Believer," *The Monkees Greatest Hits*. Arista Records, ARCD-8313, n.d.

———. 1967b. "Pleasant Valley Sunday," *The Monkees Greatest Hits*. Arista Records, ARCD-8313, n.d.

The Platters. 1958. "Twilight Time," *The Very Best of The Platters*. PolyGram Records, 314 510 317-2, 1991.

Redding, Otis. 1966. "Try a Little Tenderness," *The Very Best of Otis Redding*. Rhino Records, R2 71147, 1992.

——. 1968. "(Sittin' on) the Dock of the Bay," *The Very Best of Otis Redding*, Rhino Records, R2 71147, 1992.

The Righteous Brothers. 1965. "You've Lost That Lovin' Feelin'," *Phil Spector, Back to Mono (1958–1969)*. Phil Spector Records/Abkco Records, 7118-2, 1991.

Shaw, Sandie. 1964. "(There's) Always Something There to Remind Me," *The Look of Love, The Burt Bacharach Collection*. Warner Music Canada, WTVD 88384, 2001.

Sinatra, Frank. 1946. "Try a Little Tenderness," *The Voice of Frank Sinatra*. Columbia/Legacy, 507879-2, 2003.

——. 1960. "Try a Little Tenderness," *Nice 'n' Easy*. Capitol, 72435-33745-2-5, 2002.

Springfield, Dusty. 1964. "Wishin' and Hopin'," *The Look of Love, The Burt Bacharach Collection*. Warner Music Canada, WTVD 88384, 2001.

——. 1967. "The Look of Love," *The Look of Love, The Burt Bacharach Collection*. Warner Music Canada, WTVD 88384, 2001.

Thomas, B. J. 1969. "Raindrops Keep Fallin' on My Head," *The Look of Love, The Burt Bacharach Collection*. Warner Music Canada, WTVD 88384, 2001.

Tormé, Mel. 1946. "Try a Little Tenderness," *Jazz and Velvet*. Proper Records, Properbox 73, 2006.

——. 1957. "Try a Little Tenderness," *The Mel Tormé Collection*. Rhino Records, R2 71589, 1996.

Townshend, Pete. 1970/71. "Behind Blue Eyes" (demo version), *Scoop*. Eel Pie Recording Productions, EPR 006, 2000.

Walker Brothers. 1965. "Make It Easy on Yourself," *The Look of Love, The Burt Bacharach Collection*. Warner Music Canada, WTVD 88384, 2001.

Warwick, Dionne. 1964. "(They Long to Be) Close to You," *Make Way for Dionne Warwick*. Sequel Records, NEM CD 761, 1995.

——. 1969. "I'll Never Fall in Love Again," *The Very Best of Dionne Warwick*. Rhino Records, R2 79839, 2000.

The Who. 1971a. "Behind Blue Eyes" (previously unreleased version recorded at the Record Plant Studios, New York, March 18, 1971), *Who's Next (Deluxe Edition)*. MCA Records, 088 113 056-2, 2003.

——. 1971b. "Behind Blue Eyes" (album version), *Who's Next (Deluxe Edition)*. MCA Records, 088 113 056-2, 2003.

The Yardbirds. 1965. "For Your Love," *The Yardbirds Story*. Charly, SNAJ736CD, 2007.

The Zombies. 1968. "Time of the Season," *Odessey & Oracle*. Repertoire Records, REP 5089, 2008.

Index

Blood, Sweat & Tears 88
  "Hi-De-Ho That Old Sweet Roll"
    87–8
Blum, Stephen viii
Boone, Graeme ix
"Both Sides, Now" 5, 12–15, 89–90
Bowman, Rob 26
Breare, William 92
The Buckinghams 86, 88
  "Kind of a Drag" 88
"By the Time I Get to Phoenix" 5–8,
  12

cadence 76–7, 81
"California Girls" 48
Campbell, Glen 5–6
  "By the Time I Get to Phoenix"
    5–8, 12
Campbell, Jimmy 24
Carpenter, Karen 75–6, 80, 91, 122,
  135, 139–41
Carpenter, Richard 121–2, 125,
  133–5, 139–42
Carpenters 79–80, 122–3, 136–8,
  141–2
  "(They Long to Be) Close to You"
    77, 79, 91, 122, 133–42
  "We've Only Just Begun" 80
Chamberlain, Richard 122, 125,
  129–34, 136–8
  "(They Long to Be) Close to You"
    122, 125–6, 129–33
chest voice see register (voice)
Clayton-Thomas, David 87
"Close to You" see "(They Long to
  Be) Close to You"
Cockin, William 33, 75
Como, Perry 81–2, 85
  "Magic moments" 81–2, 85
Connelly, Reg 24
Constanten, Tom ix
Cooke, Sam 24–6, 39, 41
  "For Sentimental Reasons" 25

"Try a Little Tenderness" 24–5,
  39–41
"You Send Me" 25
Copacabana club 25
Corri, Domenico 76–7
crooners 24, 27, 29, 32–4, 38–9,
  131
Cropper, Steve 48, 52–4, 60
Crosby, Bing 24–5, 27, 31–5
  "Try a Little Tenderness" 24–39
cross-relations 51
Cummings, Burton 93–9, 102

Daltrey, Roger 117–19
"Dark Star" ix
The Dave Clark Five 86–7, 94, 97
  "Because" 94, 97
  "Do You Love Me" 86–8
David, Hal 77, 81, 121, 123–4, 126–7,
  129–30, 133, 141–2
Davis, Sheila viii, 7
DeMain, Bill 122
dénouement 18, 21
Dolenz, Mickey 77
Domenic, Serene 123
Donovan 47, 61, 63
  "Hurdy Gurdy Man" 47, 52, 61,
    63–4
"Don't Worry Baby" 90
"Do You Love Me" 86–8
dorian see modes
Dylan, Bob 47, 49, 58, 60, 77, 78
  "Girl from the North Country" 49
  "Lay Lady Lay" 47, 49, 52, 58–60,
    65
  "Positively 4th Street" 77, 78

Einarson, John 93
emphasis 23–4, 29, 31–2, 34–5, 72–3,
  81, 82, 84
Entwistle, John 116–17, 119
epilogue 15, 18
epizeuxis see rhetorical figures